DATE DUE

DEC 8 75			
FEB 8 '78			
DEC 12 79			
DEC 12 79			
JUN 17 87			
APR 27 83			

Mexico
1946-73

Mexico
1946-73

Edited by Dan Hofstadter

FACTS ON FILE, INC.   NEW YORK, N.Y.

Mexico
1946-73

Library of Congress Catalog Card Number 74-75152
ISBN 0-87196-218-7

9 8 7 6 5 4 3 2 1
PRINTED IN
THE UNITED STATES OF AMERICA

Contents

iii

Introduction

MEXICO IS ONE OF THOSE NATIONS that attract world attention over and over again because they clearly represent certain common problems or possibilities. The scene of some of the most dramatic revolutionary struggles of the 20th century, Mexico has in the past 30 years become one of the few Latin American states with a constitutional government run by duly elected civilians. Yet Mexico is more than an example: it is, with a population of nearly 50 million and a rapidly developing industrial sector, a substantial force in the Latin American world.

Mexico is beset with serious problems, however. Despite Mexico's achievement of a new social and economic stability since World War II, Mexican democracy remains a highly imperfect if no longer fragile institution. The revered constitution guarantees political freedom, and the country's revolutionary tradition promises social progress for the masses, but the federal government, dominated by a single party, often pursues policies unhampered by these difficult ideals. In recent years the nominally revolutionary government has allied itself to some of the more conservative forces in Mexican society. Mexican politicians have defended the necessity of fostering a powerful national business community to resist the inroads of U.S. industrial might. Many Mexicans are quick to assert that if it were not for the looming presence of their northern neighbor, Mexico would be a major power in the Western Hemisphere.

The Land & the People

Situated directly south of the U.S., the Republic of the United States of Mexico occupies 760,000 square miles, about $\frac{1}{4}$ the area of its northern neighbor. To the southwest lies Guatemala, to the southeast British Honduras.

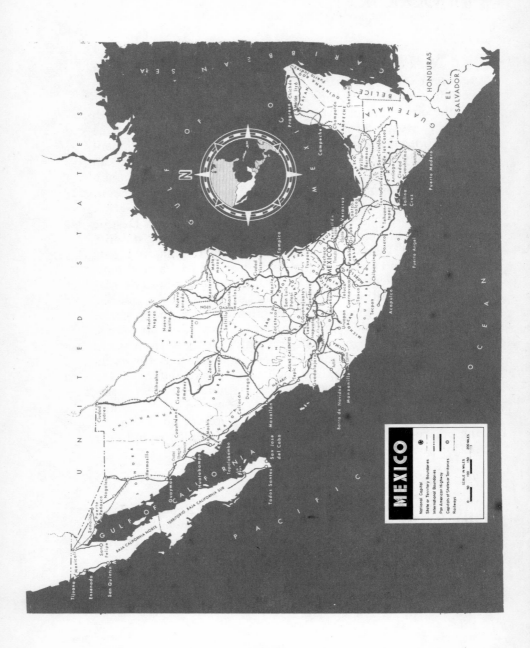

The terrain varies greatly. A depressed desert plain in the north gradually rises into a rugged upland, becoming the great central plateau, which attains 8,000 feet in elevation near Mexico City. This plateau is about 1,500 miles long and 500 miles wide. South of Mexico City begins a chain of mountains that stretches all the way to the isthmus of Tehuantepec in southernmost Mexico.

Mexico, the 3d most heavily populated country in the Western Hemisphere (after the U.S. and Brazil), had 47,267,000 inhabitants in 1967. The population (and capitals) of the principal states and territories of Mexico are:

State	Population	Capital
Aguascalientes	309,000	Aguascalientes
Baja California	966,000	Mexicali
Baja California, S.T.*	103,000	La Paz
Campeche	231,000	Campeche
Chiapas	1,512,000	Tuxtla Gutierrez
Chihuahua	1,751,000	Chihuahua
Coahuila	1,193,000	Saltillo
Colima	229,000	Colima
Distrito Federal†	7,115,000	Mexico City
Durango	939,000	Durango
Guanajuato	2,258,000	Guanajuato
Guerrero	1,570,000	Chilpancingo
Hidalgo	1,249,000	Pachuca
Jalisco	3,240,000	Guadalajara
Mexico	2,687,000	Toluca
Michoacan	2,389,000	Morelia
Morelos	571,000	Cuernavaca
Nayarit	553,000	Tepic

*Territory † Federal District

Nuevo Leon	.	.	1,605,000	Monterrey
Oaxaca	.	.	2,119,000	Oaxaca
Puebla	.	.	2,504,000	Puebla
Queretaro	.	.	455,000	Queretaro
Quintana Roo*	.	.	76,000	Chetumal
San Luis Potosi	.	.	1,395,000	San Luis Potosi
Sinaloa	.	.	1,145,000	Culiacán
Sonora	.	.	1,192,000	Hermosillo
Tabasco	.	.	667,000	Villahermosa
Tamaulipas	.	.	1,432,000	Ciudad Victoria
Tlaxcala	.	.	443,000	Tlaxcala
Veracruz	.	.	3,517,000	Jalapa
Yucatan	.	.	796,000	Merida
Zacatecas	.	.	1,056,000	Zacatecas

Half the people of Mexico live in the central part of the country around Mexico City. Migration from the often unproductive countryside has swelled the developing industrial centers. Between 1950 and 1960, for example, the population of the Federal District (the Mexico City area) increased from about 3 to about 5 million. A similar phenomenon has occurred in the northwestern region near the U.S.

About 2/3 of Mexicans are of mixed Indian and Spanish blood *(mestizos)*. The rest are for the most part pure Indian. The bulk of the purely Caucasian inhabitants is composed of a 20th-century influx of middle-class immigrants from Europe and the U.S.

Spanish is the official language, although more than 50 Indian dialects related to Mayan and Aztec are also spoken. Certain remote tribes speak only their native Indian tongues. Almost all ethnic Mexicans are Roman Catholic.

The cultural life of Mexico since 1946 has been relatively rich but perhaps not as much so as during the earlier, revolutionary period, which spawned the internationally famous Mexican school of mural-painting. One major painter raised in the mural tradition who has made a worldwide reputation is Rufino Tamayo. Perhaps the most distinguished

---

*Territory

Mexican men of letters since the war are Octavio Paz and Carlos Fuentes. Octavio Paz, a brilliant poet, has written what is perhaps the most widely admired introduction to the spirit of modern Mexico, *The Labyrinth of Solitude*. Carlos Fuentes is a sensitive left-wing novelist whose works, such as *The Death of Artemio Cruz* and *The Good Conscience*, explore the tensions between old ways and modernity and between Catholicism and modern materialism.

History to 1910

Pre-Columbian Mexico was inhabited by 2 highly civilized peoples, the Mayas and the Aztecs. Since the 1911 Revolution, the government has assiduously reminded Mexicans of their Indian background. Much that is essentially Indian remains in the culture of 20th-century Mexico. It is in many ways a misnomer to refer to Mexico as a "Latin"-American country.

The Aztec empire was overthrown in 1519 when Spanish troops under Hernan Cortes wrested Mexico from Montezuma, the Aztec monarch. The Spaniards introduced Roman Catholicism and feudalism into the country, along with the enslavement of many of the Indian inhabitants.

A long period of revolution and civil unrest began in 1810. Under the leadership of 2 priests, Miguel Hidalgo and Jose Maria Morelos, a revolution was launched against Spain. The struggle was carried on to a successful conclusion by the patriots Vicente Guerrero and Augustin Iturbide. A republic was proclaimed in 1823. But the era of violent social struggles had barely begun: it did not subside until the presidency of Avila Camacho (1940-6).

The new, poorly defended state became the prey of foreing powers. In the Mexican-American War (1846-8), Mexico lost half its territory, including New Mexico, Arizona and California, to the U.S. During a period of civil strife, Mexico was occupied by French troops (1861-7). The republic was restored and the dictator Porfirio Diaz ("*el Caudillo*," the boss) became president from 1876 (except for a brief interlude in 1880-4) until he was ovethrown in 1910-11.

Major Phases of the Mexican Revolution (1910-46)

Because of the importance of the Mexican Revolution for the history of post-World War II Mexico, a brief summary of its major phases is given below:

Madero Revolution, 1910-1—Francisco I. Madero was a wealthy and brilliant political reformer. In 1908 he had written a tract, *The Political Succession of 1910,* recommending that Porfirio Díaz, whose reelection was assured, carry out certain reforms. When Díaz snubbed him, Madero became an opposition candidate. During the election Madero was jailed. After Díaz' victory he sought refuge in the U.S., where he issued Oct. 5, 1910 his "Plan of San Luis Potosí," calling for a mass uprising against Diaz. Popular leaders such as Pancho Villa, Emiliano Zapata and Venustiano Carranza rallied behind Madero. Villa took the federal stronghold of Ciudad Juarez in May, while in the south Zapata captured Cuautla. Diaz resigned May 21, 1911 and was exiled to France.

Huerta Counter-Revolution, 1911-3—Emiliano Zapata and Pascual Orozco, another revolutionary leader, abandoned Madero for both temperamental and ideological reasons. Bernardo Reyes, a *Porfirista** general, and Felix Díaz, the ex-dictator's own nephew, slipped into Mexico to plot against the revolution. These 2 led an armed counter-revolutionary uprising Feb. 1913 (the "10 Tragic Days"), and Madero fell back on the dubious loyalty of Gen. Victoriano Huerta. Unbeknownst to Madero, U.S. Amb.-to-Mexico Henry Lane Wilson, apparently acting on his own initiative, used embassy premises to arrange a conspiratorial collusion between Díaz and Huerta. The conspirators arrested Madero and later, on U. S. government property, signed the "Pact of the Embassy" whereby Felix Diaz was to succeed Madero as president. Huerta then had Madero, the "father of the Mexican Revolu-

---

*Follower of Porfirio Diaz

tion," secretly assassinated.

Constitutionalists Against Huerta, U.S. Occupation of Veracruz, 1913-4—Huerta, the real leader of the counter-revolution, soon found himself threatened by a massive Constitutionalist alliance that included Villa, Zapata and another strongman, Alvaro Obregon. The leader of the Constitutionalists was Venustiano Carranza, who issued Mar. 1913 his "Plan of Guadalupe," calling for constitutional government. The U.S. entered the dispute when Woodrow Wilson, a sympathizer of Carranza's, become U.S. President in Mar. 1913. In an ill-conceived action aimed at helping Carranza, U.S. Marines and naval personnel occupied the port of Veracruz Apr. 21, 1914 in order to intercept a delivery of German arms to Huerta. Yet Carranza, as a patriotic Mexican, was angered by the U.S. intervention. As the situation deteriorated, with both Carranza and Huerta opposing the U.S. but still struggling against each other, a Constitutionalist army expelled Huerta from Mexico City Aug. 15, 1914. The U.S. withdrew, and Carranza uneasily took over the government.

Civil War, 1913-5—Factionalism broke out among the Constitutionalist forces, with Carranza and Obregón pitted against Villa and Zapata. Zapata was eventually subdued and Villa and his troops driven into the north.

Villa vs. Pershing, 1916—Villa then attempted to draw the U.S. into a war against Carranza by attacking the civilian population of Columbus, N.M. Mar. 9,1916. U.S. Gen. John J. Pershing invaded Mexico with an anti-Villa expeditionary force, but the quarrel was settled by Jan. 1917.

Carranza Administration, 1917-20—A constitution was finally proclaimed Feb. 5, 1917. Carranza was legally elected president Mar. 11. Much of his administration was devoted to land reform and to crushing counter-revolutionary tendencies. Carranza's succession plans led to a military *coup d'etat* in May 1920, and he was killed.

Social Revolution & Succession Problems, 1920-34—Carranza was succeeded by a squabbling triumvirate composed of Alvaro Obregon, Plutarco Elias Calles and Lazaro

Cardenas. They dominated the government even when out of office.

The following presidents held office during the years from World War I to Cárdenas' term:

President	Dates of Office
Venustiano Carranza	1915-20
Adolfo de la Muerta	1920
Alvaro Obregon	1920-4
Plutarco Elias Calles	1924-8
Emilio Portes Gil	1928-30
Pascual Ortiz Rubio	1930-2
Abelardo L. Rodriguez . . .	1932-4

All these men were of the same political faction, but bloody disturbances occurred during every succession period. The following social changes were initiated during this era: (1) the subordination of the army to the state: (2) the curbing of regional separatism; (3) the destruction of the temporal power of the Catholic Church; (4) the promotion of all-Mexican popular nationalism.

Revolutionary Revival & Cardenas, 1934-40—Lazaro Cardenas, who served as president 1934-40, was the first Mexican head of state to put major emphasis on land reform. Cardenas broke up many large estates and distributed the land to *ejidos* (communal farms). Under his leadership, Mexico again became fervently revolutionary. In 1937 Cardenas regrouped the revolutionary forces into a permanent, formal, and virtually unchallenged political party, the PRM *(Partido Revolucionario Mexicano)*, with 4 sectors—the military, the worker, the peasant, and the "popular" (middle-class) elements. Cardenas expropriated foreign oil holdings Mar. 18, 1938 (still a national holiday) and created a state oil monopoly, Pémex *(petroleos Mexicanos)*. He also nationalized the railways and vast tracts of land.

Institutional Revolution & Camacho, 1940-6—Pres. Manuel Avila Camacho concentrated on developing the PRM, which he converted into the PRI *(Partido Revolucionario Intitucional,* or Institutional Revolutionary Party) in 1946, and on strengthening democratic institutions in general. Mexico declared war on the Axis May 28, 1942 after the sinking of several of its ships in the Gulf of Mexico. Despite the formation of a strong Catholic reaction to Camacho, social peace increased markedly during his term.

The Mexican Revolution is of both great historical and emotional significance to Mexicans. The Mexican man of letters Octavio Paz summed up much of the common feeling toward the Revolution in 1950 in his book *The Labyrinth of Solitude:*

> . . . In one sense . . . the Revolution has recreated the nation; in another sense, of equal importance, it has extended nationality to races and classes which neither colonialism nor the 19th century were able to incorporate into our national life. But . . . it was incapable of creating a vital order that would be at once a world view and the basis of a really just and free society. The Revolution has not succeeded in changing our country into a community . . . . By community, I mean a world in which men recognize themselves in each other and in which the "principle of authority"—that is, force, whatever its origin and justification—concedes its place to a responsible form of liberty. . . .
>
> The Mexican Revolution was chronologically the first of the great revolutions of the 20th century. To understand it correctly, it is necessary to see it as part of a general process that is still going on. . . . It proposed to liquidate feudalism, transform the country by means of industry and technology, put an end to our economic and political dependence, and establish a genuinely democratic society. In other words, to . . . consummate at last the Independence and Reform movements and convert Mexico into a modern nation. . . . The changes were to reveal our true being, the face that was both known and unknown to us. The Revolution was going to invent a Mexico that would be faithful to itself.
>
> . . . [The Revolution] tried, within a short time and with a minimum of human sacrifices, to complete a task that had taken the European *bourgeoisie* more than 150 years. To do so, first we had to secure our political independence and recover control of our natural resources. And it had to be done without infringing on the social rights guaranteed by the Constitution of 1917. . . . In Europe and the United States these conquests were the result of over a century of proletarian struggle, and to a considerable extent they represented (and represent) participation in earnings from abroad. In Mexico we had no colonial income to distribute; we did not even own the oil, minerals, electric power and other resources with which we had to transform the country. Therefore the Revolution's problem was not merely one of beginning at the beginning: we had to begin from before the beginning. . . .
>
> The Revolution also proposed . . . to recover our natural wealth. The revolutionary governments, that of Cardenas in particular, called for the nationalization of oil, the railroads and other industries. This policy brought us into conflict with economic imperialism, and the state had to back down and suspend its expropriations, though without surrendering what had already been recovered. (. . . Our industrial growth would have been impossible without the nationalization of the petroleum industry.) The Revolution . . .

created new state industries by means of a network of banks and credit institutions, gave financial and technical assistance to others (private and semi-
private), and in general tried to guide out economic development rationally
and for the benefit of the public. . . . The face of Mexico began to change.
. . . Little by little a new working class and a *bourgeoisie* arose. Both
classes lived in the shadow of the state and have only now begun to achieve
an autonomous life.

    . . . We are still far from achieving everything that is needed. We do
not have any basic industries except for the beginnings of a steel industry; . . .
we are still short of roads, bridges and railways; we have turned our backs
on the sea, and lack ports, vessels and a fishing industry; our foreign exchange is balanced only because of tourism and the dollars our seasonal
workers send back from the United States. And the fact that North American
capital . . . is increasingly more powerful in the vital centers of our economy is even more decisive. Essentially, then, we are still a country producing raw materials, despite a certain amount of industrial growth. . . . In
foreign trade we are subject to the fluctuations of the world markets, and . . .
at home we suffer from instability, poverty and a cruel difference in the lives
of the rich and the poor.

Single Party Rule

    The Mexican government is organized analogously to
that of the U.S., with a bicameral legislature (the Senate and
the Chamber of Deputies, together known as the Congress), a
strong executive (the president) and a Supreme Court. Perhaps
the major difference is that the Mexican chief of state has
inherited some of the authority of the old *caudillos* (autocrats)
like Porfirio Diaz. The president is expected to (and does)
wield his power rather heavily, but he is not allowed to run
for reelection. Mexican presidents serve for 6 years.

    The major governmental difference between the U.S.
and Mexico, however, is the persistence in Mexico of a
working single-party system. The PRI *(Partido Revolucionario
Institucional,* Party of Revolutionary Institutions or Institutional Revolutionary Party) always returns an overwhelming
majority to Congress and never fails to have its presidential
candidate elected. Opposition parties are permitted to exist, as
long as they are not deemed subversive, but they have never
fared well in national elections.

    The government party was formed in 1929 to group
together various revolutionary organizations. It was original-
ly known as the PNR *(Partido Nacional Revolutionario); in*

1937 it became the PRM *(Partido de la Revolucion Mexicana)*
and in 1946 it assumed its present name, the PRI. Perhaps
the most distinctive feature of the PRI is its division into 3
"sectors": labor, peasant and "popular" *(i.e.,* heterogeneous
middle-class). To each sector is allotted a number of deputies
to Congress; the 3 sectors together choose a presidential
candidate acceptable to all.

The PRI is essentially a political "machine," somewhat
similar to the "machine" parties that for years have controlled certain urban wards in the U.S. The success of the
PRI is a result not so much of the intimidation of rivals—
although that occurs—as of a cleverly applied policy of "co-
optation" whereby new political pressure or reform groups
are incorporated into the party and allowed a measure of
power. Traditionally the "machine" has served best the interests of industrial workers. In recent years, however, as a
consequence of the pressure for industrial and commercial
growth, the PRI has largely come to represent the industrial
bourgeoisie of the Mexico City area and certain northern
centers.

An interesting comment on the PRI and on Mexico's
political process was made by the staff of the U.S. Senate
Foreign Relations Committee in a study dated Sept. 18,
1967:

> The great contribution of the Mexicans to political development is the
> PRI *(Partido Revolucionario Institucional)*, which for a generation has
> brought the country peace, steady economic growth and orderly govern-
> mental transition.
>
> What is so ingenious about the PRI is the way in which it accom-
> modates the Latin American temperament with the demands of a moderniz-
> ing society. The PRI is centralized, authoritarian and paternalistic. The pres-
> ident of the republic is the undisputed *jefe,* leader, *caudillo.* He selects or
> approves PRI candidates for Congress, for governor, for mayor. The Mexican
> Congress has never been known to say him nay, or even to delay very long
> in doing his bidding.
>
> At the same time, the PRI is eclectic and broadly representative of
> diverse interest groups. Its members cover an ideological spectrum ranging
> from conservative to near-Marxist. The party holds this disparate collection
> together through being responsive to trends of public opinion, through
> memory of the chaos which afflicted Mexico in the days before the PRI,
> through the practical difficulties of achieving political success outside the
> PRI framework, and at times through old-fashioned, hard-nosed party

discipline—those who don't go along, at least up to a point, don't get along.
For those who do go along, and who assess the prevailing winds correctly,
the PRI provides opportunity for political and economic advancement.

Further, one of the foundation stones of the Mexican revolution—the
principle of no reelection—insures that there is a constant turnover among
political leaders. In the Mexican context, this has 2 great advantages:
(1) It means that there is always room for the advancement of new, young
talent; and (2) it means that no administration can perpetuate itself in power.
As Frank Bradenburg has put it in a perceptive comment, "Mexicans avoid
personal dictatorship by retiring their dictators every 6 years."[1] Mexicans
tolerate as a lesser evil the fact that this also intensifies graft toward the end
of an administration, because the ins know that they have to get it then or not
at all. Mexican ex-presidents join a select group of the revolutionary
family—an extralegal council of elders whose most important function is
selecting the presidential successor. Incoming Mexican presidents are thus
obligated to all of their living predecessors. Although incoming presidents
bring their own team to power with them, there is not a complete change in
the 2d and 3d echelons of PRI leadership. The constitutional prohibition of
reelection applies only to the office which one is holding at a given time.
Thus, one may switch from House to Senate in Congress, from Congress to
a governorship, or vice versa. Care is usually taken, however, to see to it
that enough jobs open up to keep new blood flowing in.

Left-Wing Opposition

Mexico is, officially, a "revolutionary" society, the
very word being incorporated into the name of the ruling
political party. Since the end of World War II, however,
Mexico has edged further and further from its original revolutionary ideals, partly, no doubt, because some of them
have been accomplished. Thus the ruling PRI has left considerable room for meaningful opposition from the left. The
Moscow-oriented Mexican Communist Party itself has never
counted more than 30,000 members at the very most, but
other less ideologically clear-cut groups have sprung up since
Cuba's Castro revolution.

For many years the most influential of Mexican radicals
was Vicente Lombardo Toledano. Born of Creole parents
in 1894, Lombardo Toledano abandoned a brilliant academic
career early in the Revolution to become a labor organizer.
He created a massive labor coalition of workers and peasants

---

[1] Frank Brandenburg, "The Relevance of Mexican Experience to Latin
American Development." *Orbis*, Vol. IX, No. 1 (Spring 1965), p. 194.

in 1933. This coalition backed Lombardo Toledano's friend Lazaro Cardenas in his struggle for the presidency and became the official pro-government labor union in 1935. It styled itself the Federation of Mexican Workers *(Confederacion de Trabajadores Mexicanos,* or CTM).

The Cardenas epoch (1934-40) was Mexico's most left-leaning phase since the days of Villa and Zapata. It was also Lombardo Toledano's heyday. As the PRM (later PRI) became more moderate under Manuel Avila Camacho and Miguel Aleman Valdes, Lombardo Toledano began to run more and more afoul of the government. Camacho ousted Lombardo Toledano from the leadership of the CTM, and by June 1943, when the Soviets set up a suspiciously over-staffed embassy in Mexico City, the deposed labor boss was courting Soviet Amb. Constantine Oumansky and his Mexican Stalinist friends. Although no evidence has been produced that Lombardo Toledano was ever a memeber of Mexico's tiny Communist party, by 1947 he was clearly associated with the Moscow party line, from which he rarely deviated. Lombardo Toledano founded a new Marxist party, the *Partido Popular,* in 1948. His attempt to lure the CTM into this new group resulted in his expulsion from that organization. The *Partido Popular,* with the backing of other left-wing groups, ran Lombardo Toledano against Ruiz Cortines in the 1952 elections, but he did rather poorly. Stalinism, both as an international force and in Mexico, waned in the 1950s, and Lombardo Toledano never regained his former prestige.

Catholic Opposition

Anti-clericalism is written into the Mexican Constitution of 1917. Until the Camacho administration, Mexican revolutionaries tended to consider the Vatican and the Mexican Catholic Church hierarchy as a counter-revolutionary force.

PRM presidential candidate Avila Camacho was bitterly challenged in the 1940 elections by Juan Andreu Almazan, the nominee of the opposition *Partido de Accion Nacional*

(PAN), which had heavy Catholic backing. After Camacho defeated Almazan, bloody riots broke out between supporters of the 2 candidates. The upshot of these riots was the rapid growth of a subversive right–wing Catholic movement known as *Sinarquismo*.

The *Sinarquista* movement *(Sinarquismo,* or "sinarchism," was a neologism coined to stand for social order, *i.e.,* the opposite of anarchism) was actually founded in 1947 but attracted most of its adherents in the wake of Camacho's victory. Popular among rural Catholics and certain northern businessmen, the *Sinarquistas* virtually took over Leon, in the state of Guanajuato, provoking the publication of the anti-*Sinarquist* Espionage Law of Sept. 1941. The *Sinarquistas* were by-and-large right-wing extremists, pro-Franco if not pro-Axis, and eager to establish a Catholic theocracy in Mexico.

Juan Ignacio Padilla (no relation to the Ezequiel Padilla who ran on the PDM ticket against Miguel Aleman in 1946) became the *Sinarquista* leader in 1951. He softened the party stand in 1952 and endorsed the presidential candidate of PAN. Despite this attempt to abandon its subversive role and enter the mainstream of the nation's political life, *Sinarquismo* dwindled to a minor political phenomenon in the early 1950s.

The major reason for the ebbing of this radical Catholic opposition was the rapprochement taking place in Mexico between the PRI and the Church. Although Church and state remained rigidly separate, Pres. Camacho did much to heal wounded Catholic feelings by his famous pronouncement *"Yo soy creyente"* ("I am a believer"). The same tactic was repeated in 1958 by Adolfo Lopez Mateos, who openly touted his Catholicism, but by this time hardly anybody was shocked. Only a small minority of Mexicans could remember the power of the Church before 1910, and even faraway Rome itself seemed permeated by the new "ecumenical" liberalism.

By now the Catholic Church, although still not a major force in Mexican politics, is once again an accepted and recognized feature of Mexican life.

Economy

Althought over half the Mexican labor force is employed in farming, forestry, fishing and hunting, most of Mexico's gross national product (GNP) comes from mining, crude oil extraction and refining, industry, tourism and international trade. Mexico is self-sufficient in most agricultural products with the exception of meat and dairy foods. Mexico's chief agricultural exports by value are cotton, sugar and coffee.

An important sector of Mexican industry in devoted to developing the nation's substantial oil resources. Special complications have arisen in the oil industry because of the nationalization of Mexico's oil resources in 1938 and the formation the state petroleum monopoly, Pemex *(Petroleos Mexicanas)*.

Mexico is a major mining nation. It is the world's 2d producer of silver and sulphur and has vast resources of lead, copper and zinc.

The Mexican economy has grown with speed in the past 20 years. The annual rate of increase in the GNP from 1950 to 1965 for example was 6% (adjusted for price changes). The sectors that grew the most rapidly in the 1960s were commerce, manufacturing, the generation of electricity, petroleum extraction and refining and tourism. Mining, fishing, agriculture and construction lagged.

The shift from an economy based on agriculture and mining to a more diversified one with a larger industrial sector has been a major aim of every Mexican government from Miguel Aleman Valdes to Luis Echeverria Alvarez. At the same time, however, the government has tried to discourage Mexico's high percentage of the agricultual under-employed from continuing its massive influx into the larger metropolitan concentrations.

Until recently mining was Mexico's most substantial source of exports. In 1939, for example, minerals accounted for 65% of the value of all exports; minerals' share of total exports was down to 17% by 1965. Other major exported items include industrial products, cotton, coffee, sugar, fish and meat. About 60% of Mexico's exported value goes to the U.S., which also accounts for 66% of Mexico's imports. Mexico still sustains a substantial (and widening) trade deficit. Earnings from tourism compensate largely for the trade gap.

Labor

The Mexican labor force is heavily concentrated in agriculture. The distribution of the labor force in 1965 was: agriculture 53%, manufacturing 17%, services 13%, community services 9%, other 8%. 32.3% of the total population was in the labor force in 1965. 30% of this labor force, however, was underemployed, and $1\frac{1}{2}$% was unemployed, according to government figures.

Under Article 123 of the constitution, every employe is entitled to: one paid day of rest after 6 of work; 5 paid holidays annually, 4 days of vacation after the first year of employment and 6 days after every subsequent year. Usually, 90% of the employes of any Mexican firm must be Mexican citizens.

Mixed commissions representing labor, management and the government fix the minimum wage rates in every locality. The minimum daily wage for 1958 in the Federal District was 12 pesos for urban workers and $10\frac{1}{2}$ for agricultural workers.

The labor sector is as a whole chaotically structured by comparison with U.S. labor. The left-centrist labor unions are collectively known as the BUO (Bloque de Unidad Obrera, or United Labor Bloc). This grouping represents about 85% of the total labor sector. Actually, however, only about 19% of the total labor force is unionized, largely because the PRI-dominated government has prohibited the entry of civil servants and agricultural laborers' affiliations into the BUO. The largest union within the BUO is the CTM (Confederacion de Trabajadores Mexicanos, or Federation of Mexican

Workers). The CTM's subgroups—unlike the AFL-CIO's vertical and horizontal unions—are organized on the basis of region rather than trade or craft.

The non-BUO unions are generally more left-wing in outlook. These unions, however, often cooperate with the BUO unions, and in the last several decades the entire issue of left/right political orientation within the labor movement has become blurred. The largest non-BUO union is the CROC *(Confederación Revolucionario de Obreros y Campesinos,* or Revolutionary Federation of Workers & Peasants), which was organized in 1952 from several left-leaning groups. The CTM is still considerably more powerful than the CROC.

The CTM since the early 1950s has been affiliated with the ORIT *(Organisación Regional Inter-Americana de Trabajadores,* or Inter-American Regional Organization of Workers) and the ICFTU (International Confederation of Free Trade Unions). Membership in the AFL and CIO (later the AFL-CIO) has been vigorously rejected. (The AFL-CIO itself withdrew from the ICFTU in Jan. 1969.)

Estimates of union membership from the latter part of the Diaz Ordaz period (1964-70) put BUO membership at 1.9 million and non-BUO membership at about 240,000. Membership of the major unions:

CTM (Federation of Mexican Workers), BUO . . .		1,500,000
CROC (Revolutionary Confederation of Workers &		
Peasants), non-BUO		150,000
STFRM (Railroad Workers' Union), BUO . . .		102,000
STMMSRM (Mining & Metal Workers' Union), BUO . .		90,000
STPRM (Petroleum Workers' Union), BUO		80,000

There has been a significant though decreasing migration of Mexican seasonal agricultural workers *(braceros)* into the U.S. under a now discontinued agreement with Washington. Significant problems have arisen because of the frequency of illegal border-crossings. The illegal immigrants are popularly known in the Southwestern U.S. as "wetbacks," because many swim or wade the Rio Grande to cross the international frontier. It is reported that an important part of Mexico's dollar reserves came from the earnings of *braceros.*

The *bracero* program had begun in 1942 when Mexico agreed to contribute to the growing U.S. labor shortage caused by U.S.' entry into World War II. After the war, migrant workers continued to seek employment in the U.S. under the protection of the Farm Labor section of the U.S. Department of Labor as authorized by Public Law 78. The original *bracero* program was terminated in 1964. Migrant labor both legal and illegal, however, has continued to flow into the U.S. from Mexico under a variety of conditions.

Agrarianism

Mexico is still predominantly an agricultural society. It is largely self-sufficient agriculturally, and about half of its export earning comes from agriculture. This fact has 2 immediate consequences: (1) the economy is critically open to weather fluctuations and disasters *(e.g.,* droughts and floods in 1967 destroyed 35% of the country's major export commodity, cotton); (2) the peasants have a significant say within the ruling party, the PRI, and tend toward the classically conservative peasant orientation.

53% of the Mexican work force is active in agriculture. The government has tried to increase productivity and growth in this sector in several ways: (1) land reform; (2) rural credit programs; (3) rural construction and irrigation; (4) agronomy and seed improvements.

A distinctive feature of Mexican agrarianism is the *ejido.* This form of rural cooperative, somewhat similar to the Soviet *sovkhoz,* was an outgrowth of the rural upheaval of the Cardenas period. In the *ejido,* the arable land is owned not by the state but by *ejido* members themselves, either as a collectivity or as individuals with titles to separate land parcels. Cardenas' successor Avila Camacho extended the *ejido* program both by forming new *ejidos* and by redistributing better land to *ejidos* old and new. By the beginning of Miguel Aleman's presidential term in 1946, the *ejidos* were a fixture in Mexican rural life. 60% of the total cropland belonged to *ejidos,* and over 2 million Mexicans lived off the earnings of this land. There have been further land redistribution programs favoring the *ejidos* between 1946 and 1973, notably a 1962 agrarian reform, but they have not been particularly extensive.

Popular Sector

A distinguishing feature of Mexico is the PRI-affiliated Popular Sector, an increasingly powerful organization of essentially middle-class groups. This sector has been organized to integrate the middle-class into the framework of "revolutionary institutions," the theme of class struggle having been dropped from the PRI platform in 1946. The Popular Sector cooperates with the peasant and labor sectors within the PRI. The sector includes: bureaucrats' unions (FSTSE), teachers (SNTE), cooperatives, smallholders (CNPPA, ANC), small businessmen and industrialists, professionals, intellectuals, youth groups (CJM, etc.), artisans, women's organizations (STP, MR, MM, etc.), diversified persons. The total membership is almost 2 million.

Foreign Policy

Relations with the U.S. have improved markedly since Mexico, in 1942, joined the Allies in World II.

Major factors in this improvement have been: (1) the increasing *embourgeoisement* of the Mexican revolutionary government; (2) a marked rise in U.S. tourism to Mexico; (3) the return of Mexican war trophies by the U.S. following the Aleman-Truman visits of 1946; (4) the return of the Chamizal border area to Mexico in 1967; (5) the settlement of the *bracero* question in 1964.

Disputes continue, however, over the issues of shrimp fishing and off-shore territorial limits, Colorado River oversalinity, the restriction of cotton imports to the U.S. and the attempted interception of marijuana smugglers, which obstructs the flow of U.S. tourists across the U.S.-Mexico border.

Certain of these seemingly trivial issues have been of

vital concern to Mexicans. The return of the war trophies (battle standards, etc.), for example, was greatly appreciated by the Mexican people. The Chamizal border area, of minimal interest to most U.S. citizens, was announced with banner headlines in Mexico. Finally, the bungled surveillance of the U.S.-Mexican border (Operation Intercept, begun Sept. 21, 1969) caused major losses to Mexican tourism and was finally abandoned at the bequest of Pres. Gustavo Diaz Ordaz.

Mexico is a member of the OAS (Organization of American States) but has disagreed with the U.S. frequently on OAS issues. Mexico has abstained from or, opposed most OAS resolutions against Castro's Cuba. Mexico, however, did support the OAS' "Cuban missile" resolution against the stationing of Soviet missile bases in the Westren Hemisphere.

Despite its neutral stand in the hostility between Cuba and the U.S., the Mexican government was not unaware of a sharp rise in Mexican tourist earnings following the closing of Havana as a vacation and gambling center for U.S. tourists.

Mexico is a signatory of the Inter-American Treaty of Reciprocal Assistance and a member of the UN, LAFTA (Latin-American Free Trade Association) and the Alliance for Progress. Mexico's adherence to the Inter-American Treaty commits it to defend any American sovereign state attacked by a non-hemispheric power. This makes Mexico and the U.S. defensive allies. But Mexico interprets the principles of self-determination and non-intervention quite literally. Accordingly Mexico has stayed out of the U.S.-Cuban dispute except during the installation of Soviet missiles in Cuba, which Mexico interpreted as a threat to hemispheric solidarity.

Mexico receives a large amount of foreign financing in various forms. The principal sources of foreign capital are U.S. loans and grants (from the Export-Import Bank, Social Progress Trust Fund, AID [Agency for International Development], Food for Freedom, military assistance programs, etc.). For the fiscal years 1946-65, U.S. government assistance to

Mexico totalled about $1 billion (over half in Import-Export Bank loans).

International agencies have often given Mexico extensive loans (for example, a total of $231 million in 1966). Major sources of the loans are the IBRD (International Bank for Reconstruction & Development), International Finance Corp., Inter-American Development Bank, UNDP (UN Development Program) Special Fund, etc.

Mexico has also received substantial aid from Canada, Italy and West Germany. The bulk has come from Canada, especially from 1960 to 1966 (almost $80 million).

THE NARRATIVE IN THIS BOOK begins with the post-World War II election campaign that made Miguel Aleman Valdes president of Mexico. It continues through the Ruiz Cortines, Lopez Mateos and Diaz Ordaz administrations and on into the Echeverria administration. Much of the material is adapted from the record compiled by FACTS ON FILE. As in all FACTS ON FILE books, great pains were taken to present all facts without bias.

ALEMAN ADMINISTRATION, 1946-52

Miguel Aleman Valdes was the first Mexican president to put major government emphasis on industrialization. Under him Mexico definitively entered a post-revolutionary phase. Private entrepreneurs and foreign capitalists gained new influence, and Pemex, the state petroleum monopoly, finally became an effeciently run concern.

But Aleman had become one of Mexico's least popular presidents by 1952. He antoganized *ejidarios* by his failure to support the *ejido* program, and he alienated organized labor by his tough handling of dissident oil workers. He was widely regarded as a grafter who had enriched himself at the expense of both the Mexican people and the big businessmen on whom he relied to help industrialize the nation.

One of Aleman's contributions to Mexican progress, however, was his continuation of an anti-illiteracy campaign that had been launched in 1944 by Aleman's predecessor, Pres. Avila Camacho (1940-6). Aleman continued to set up thousands of anti-illiteracy centers throughout Mexico. Many were aimed at the so-called "monolinguals," Indians who spoke only some unwritten Indian dialect and no Spanish. The tribes were taught to read first their own language, spelled phonetically, and then Spanish.

Mexico's Public Education Ministry reported Aug. 21, 1947 that one million Mexicans had learned to read since the beginning of the anti-illiteracy campaign in 1944. The ministry said Dec. 1, 1947 that 350,000 adults had learned how to read in 1947 and that 100,000 had been taught in the previous 4 months alone.

2 noteworthy institutional changes took place during the Aleman administration:

(1) The right to vote in municipal elections and the right to hold municipal offices were extended to married women 18 and older and to unmarried women 21 and older

31

Jan. 1, 1947.

(2) The Mexican Congress Dec. 20, 1951 approved the establishment of the 29th Mexican state, to be called Baja California (Lower California). The new state was located in the northern part of the peninsula of Baja California directly below the U.S. state of California. Previously Baja California had been a federal territory, and the smaller (southern) part of the peninsula continued as such. The new state included the cities of Tijuana and Mexicali, and like other states was entitled to elect 2 senators. Being sparsely populated, however, Baja California could send only one deputy to the Chamber of Deputies. Tijuana was selected as the state capital.

Born in Sayula, Veracruz, in 1902, the son of Gen. Miguel Aleman, Miguel Aleman Valdes had received his law degree from the National University of Mexico in 1928. He served as a member of the higher tribunal of justice and was governor of Veracruz state 1936-40. He directed the presidential campaign of Manuel Avila Camacho and was Camacho's minister of the interior *(secretario de gobernación)* 1940-5. Aleman, the youngest of Camacho's ministers and the one most responsible for the country's wartime stability, was regarded then as a moderate, conciliatory man with great political shrewdness.

Alemán Elected President

The most orderly Mexican presidential elections to date took place July 7, 1946. Victory was virtually assured to Miguel Aleman Valdes, since he was the choice of the ruling government party, the PRI *(Partido Revolucionario Institucional)*. Yet candidates from several other parties seriously challenged the 2-decade-old supremacy of the PRI. The major opposition came from Ezequiel Padilla of the newly created PDM *(Partido Democratico Mexicana);* there were also 2 candidates who represented a rather limited constituency among professional military men, Gen. Castro of the Mexican Constitutional Party and Gen. Calderon of the Revolutionary

Revindication Party.

The presidential vote in the various regions:

	Vote			Percentage within Region		
Region	Aleman	Padilla	Castro and Calderon	Aleman	Padilla	Castro and Calderon
Core . . .	971,407	262,737	35,716	76.3	20.7	2.8
South . . .	286,240	43,002	4,324	85.9	13.0	1.2
West . . .	165,874	42,327	11,414	75.8	19.3	5.2
North . . .	363,904	95,350	16,308	76.1	20.0	3.4
Republic . .	1,787,425	443,416	67,762	77.8	19.2	3.0
Federal District	126,646	88,826	6,666	51.9	39.9	3.0

The presidential campaign had begun as early as May 1945. The leaders of the PRM (later the PRI) "machine" gathered secretly May 24, 1945 to pick a candidate for the presidency. According to this informal arrangement, known as the "Pact of the Centrals," Alemán was to be groomed first as a "pre-candidate" and finally nominated by the party. Thus Aleman's election to the most powerful position in Mexico was virtually certain a full 14 months before the actual polling. Aleman then resigned as interior minister to pick a campaign a staff and draw up a platform.

A PRM national convention took place in Mexico City Jan. 18, 1946 and formally nominated candidates for the national and state elections. As planned Aleman was nominated for president. (It was during this meeting that the PRM reconstituted itself as the PRI). On being nominated, Aleman presented to the 1967 delegates his platform, called the "plan Aleman." The platform emphasized industrialization and social harmony; the traditional call for "class struggle" was omitted.

Aleman's principal opponent, Ezequiel Padilla, had previously served as foreign minister in Camacho's cabinet. He resigned from his post July 11, 1945 and asked those who had been boosting him as a future presidential candidate to refrain from rhetoric until he could defend his international policies. The Democratic Party nominated Padilla Nov. 24 as presidential candidate. The PRM (PRI) assailed him as the "candidate of the U.S," and labor leader. Vicente Lombardo Toledano charged him several times with being in league with the right-wing Sinarquist Union.

The U.S. State Department Dec. 18, 1945 ordered U.S. Amb.-to-Mexico George S. Messersmith to investigate charges by Lombardo Toledano that "certain Yankee imperialist companies" were smuggling arms to the Sinarquist Union in Mexico. Lombardo Toledano Dec. 19 reaffirmed his charges, including that of "illicit" U.S. support to Padilla. The State Department said Dec. 21 that Manuel Tello, Mexican undersecretary for foreign affairs, had told Messersmith that Mexico did not "support the statements of Lombardo Toledano" and would investigate the matter futher. Meanwhile, the Sinarquist Union sued Lombardo Toledano Dec. 22 for slander. Padilla told a Democratic Party meeting in Cuernavaca Dec. 23 that Lombardo Toledano's charge of support from U.S. interests was false. Ramon Beteta Quintana, former undersecretary of the treasury and currently campaign manager for Alemán, also said in Mexico City Dec. 27 that he had "no knowledge whatsoever" of U.S. government or private intervention in favor of Padilla.

3 people were killed and 86 wounded in clashes in Cuernavaca and nearby towns Dec. 23 between Padillistas and supporters of Alemán.

During the campaign both Alemán and Padilla advocated progressive domestic social policies and friendship with the U.S. Padilla's main support was among middle-class farmers and workers, not in the big pro-government labor organization, the BUO *(Bloque de Unidad Obrera)*.

The elections of July 7 were the first to be supervised under a new system of local electoral commissions each consisting of 3 independent citizens and 2 members of political parties. These commissions had been formed under the provisions of an Electoral Law promulgated by Pres. Avila Camacho Dec. 1945. (Previous elections had suffered from severe abuses in the hands of local municipal councils.) Between $2\frac{1}{2}$ and 3 million Mexicans had registered to vote beginning Feb. 14. The franchise was held by all Mexican males over 21, women not then having the right to vote.

The election was the first entirely pacific one in Mexican

history. (In the previous election, in 1940, 47 people had been killed and 300 injured.) After the final count July 14, Padilla formally conceded the election to Aleman, although protesting certain irregularities and violations of the Electoral Law of 1945 by the ruling PRI. Police Aug. 6, however, arrested 8 persons for an alleged plot to assassinate Pres.-elect Alemán and Sen.-elect Carlos Serrano. The War Department reported later Aug. 22 that troops had been called into the Tres Valles quarter of Veracruz after political disputes had resulted in 6 killings.

Observers noted the following facts about the 1946 elections: (1) Aleman was the first civilian to become head-of-state in Mexico since the murder of Mexican revolutionary hero Francisco I. Madero in 1913. (2) The principal defeated candidate, Ezequiel Padilla, did not attempt to contest the election results by force (a common occurence after prewar elections. (3) A genuine loyal opposition emerged, with the election to the Chamber of Deputies of several non-PRM candidates, including 2 millionaires, a *Sinarquista* and 4 others.

Lombardo Toledano commented after the elections: "First [*i.e.,* after the 1910 Revolution] the generals got together in conclaves to decide who would be the president. Then the governors did the same thing. A little later the labor organizations distributed the posts. Today the actions of citizens say the word."

Aleman was inaugurated Dec. 1, 1946. He said in his inaugural address that the "Good Neighbor" policy "satisfies our ideals of international understanding," and he held that "the new world must be the guardian of human freedoms" His cabinet: *Foreign Affairs*—Jaime Torres Bodet; *Interior*—Hector Perez Martinez: *Treasury*—Ramon Beteta; *Education*—Manuel Gual Vidal; *Agriculture*—Nazario Ortiz Garza; *Public Health & Welfare*—Dr. Rafael Pascasio Jamboa; *National Defense*—Gen. Gilberto R. Limon; *Communications & Public Works*—Augustin Garcia Lopez; *National Economy*—Antonio Ruiz Galindo; *Labor & Social Welfare*—Andres Serra Rojas; *Acting Secretary of the Navy*—Rear Adm. Luis Schaufelberger

de la Torre; *Attorney General*—Francisco Gonzalez de la Vega;
Governor of the Federal District—Sen. Fernando Casas Aleman;
Agrarian Department Chief—Mario Souza; *District Attorney of
the Federal District*—Carlos Franco Sodi; *Irrigation*—Adolfo
Orive de Alba; *National Lands & Administrative Inspection*—
Alfonso Caso.

(The cabinet did not remain unchanged for Aleman's
entire term. A minor cabinet change took place Oct. 8, 1948:
Commodore David Coello Ochoa was appointed as navy
secretary (vacant since Aleman's inauguration and a minor
ministry because of the small size of the Mexican navy);
Manuel Ramirez Vasquez was promoted from undersecretary
to secretary of labor and social welfare, replacing Andres
Serra Rojas, who had resigned in 1947.)

In his inauguration and first official policy statement,
Aleman advocated more protective tariffs for Mexican industries, a campaign against inflation and a new irrigation
project to extend over about 3½ million acres.

U.S.-MEXICAN RELATIONS

Aleman & Truman Reaffirm 'Good Neighbor' Policy

Aleman's first major act as president was to reaffirm
his country's friendship for the U.S. Many observers held that
this was in keeping with his general strategy of playing down
the "proletarian" or "revolutionary" character of the Mexican
government.

Aleman and U.S. Pres. Harry S. Truman exchanged
visits to each others' capital cities early in 1947. No visits
by heads of state had previously taken place between the 2
nations.

Truman made the first visit, landing in Mexico City
Mar. 3. Truman laid a wreath on the statue of the Ninos of
Chapultepec (martyred cadets of the Mexican-American war),
thereby signifying his friendship for the Mexican people.
The gesture was reported to have had a favorable effect
among the people of Mexico City. Truman returned to

Washington Mar. 6.

An all-out official Washington reception launched Aleman on a 9-day U.S. visit Apr. 29. He arrived from Mexico City in Truman's plane *Sacred Cow,* accompanied by Foreign Min. Jaime Tórres Bodet, Finance Secy. Ramon Beteta and U.S. Amb.-to-Mexico Walter Thurston. Truman headed the greeters at National Airport, then gave a White House state dinner at which he said: "If we could just get friendship and unity in the Eastern Hemisphere, we would have no more trouble."

During Aleman's visit he and Truman issued a joint communique in which they emphasized further bilateral co-operation and specified that the U.S. would help Mexico with loans and with the stabilization of the peso. In return, Mexico was to back the main drift of U.S. foreign policy. (Despite the "revolutionary" character of the Mexican regime, left-wing Mexicans tended to maintain a distinct coldness toward Soviet attempts to export the Russian brand of Marxism. Many Mexicans asserted that their own home-grown form of modern revolution needed no foreign advice or interference. Hence, Mexicans like Aleman were not averse to backing the U.S. as the "cold war" deepened.)

The 2 visits were officially termed non-political. In a speech to a special joint session of the U.S. Congress, however, Aleman reaffirmed Mexico's adherence to the "Good Neighbor" policy. Aleman also emphasized Mexico's ambition to be an equal partner of the U.S. in hemispheric matters.

When Aleman returned from Washington May 7 he was greeted by an enormous demonstration in Mexico City. This popular jubilation was seconded May 14 by a delegation of living Mexican ex-presidents.

These terms of U.S.-Mexican financial agreements were announced by the 2 governments May 13: (1) the U.S. would buy $50 million worth of pesos by July 1, 1951 to stabilize the dollar-peso exchange rate set up in Nov. 1941; (2) the Export-Import Bank would lend Mexico $50 million to finance development projects of "greatest and earliest contribution" to the Mexican economy.

In accordance with a proclaimed policy of protecting Mexican industries, however, Aleman June 23 created a committee to supervise foreign investments and decreed that foreign investors may not hold more than 49% interest in any Mexican enterprise. U.S. investors were the principal foreigners affected by the decree.

Mexico Signs Hemisphere Treaty

The Inter-American Treaty of Reciprocal Assistance (also known as the Treaty of Rio de Janeiro) was signed by 103 delegates representing Mexico and 19 other western hemisphere nations at the Itamaraty Palace (location of the Brazilian foreign office) in Rio de Janeiro Sept. 2, 1947. A principal feature of the treaty as far as Mexico was concerned was that, in effect, it tied Mexico to the U.S. in a mutual security arrangement.

The treaty provided for: (1) peaceful settlement, short of UN intervention, of disputes between Western Hemisphere nations; (2) united defense against aggression under an agreement that "an armed attack . . . against an American state shall be considered as an attack against all American states . . ." In Articles 1-6 the Rio Treaty condemned war and the "threat or use of force in any manner inconsistent with" the UN Charter; pledged efforts to settle all disputes between signatory nations peacefully, before they are referred to the UN; agreed on joint defense of any American nation attacked within its own territory; defined the Western Hemisphere defense zone; allowed for joint action against aggressions that have not reached the shooting stage. Article 7 prescribed that if fighting broke out between American states, they might be called on to suspend hostilities and "restore the status quo ante bellum" pending peaceful adjustment: "Rejection of the pacifying action will be considered in the determination of an aggressor . . ." Article 8 specified actions that might be taken against an aggressor (diplomatic or economic sanctions or armed force). Article 9 further defined aggressions: unprovoked armed attack against "the territory, the people or the land, sea or air forces of another state"; armed invasion that violates legal boundaries or "a region which is under the effective jurisdiction of another state." Thus the treaty may be invoked when American interests outside the Western Hemisphere are jeopardized.

The Treaty of Rio de Janeiro became operative Dec. 3, 1948, after the requisite number of ratifications.

Mexico & U.S. Erase Animal Disease

An outstanding U.S.-Mexican problem was the persistane of hoof-and-mouth disease in the livestock-rearing sections of Mexico, such as the states of Tabasco and Michoacan. This contagious animal disease affected the feet and mouths of steer raised for beef. Following the Aleman-Truman talks of March-May 1947, a U.S.-Mexican Joint Commission on Hoof-and-Mouth Disease was set up.

Aleman noted in his first annual report to Congress Sept. 1, 1947, that hoof-and-mouth disease had reached epidemic proportions and that it was currently his administration's most pressing problem.

There were 2 reasons the U.S. was willing to spend considerable sums to conquer this disease: (1) To prevent the possible spread of the disease to Texas and the U.S. Southwest; (2) to fill the need for cheap beef in sections of Europe that the U.S. was committed to defend. (The U.S. later purchased Mexican beef for export to Europe.)

Joint Commission veterinarian teams toured the Mexican countryside during the summer and fall of 1947. Their major goal was to slaughter all animals afflicted with the disease. By late July the commission reported having killed 168,000 animals worth $8 million in its attempt to eradicate the epidemic. Sporadic resistence to the teams from *campesinos* (peasants) was reported. The worst incident occurred in late August in Ciudad Hidalgo, Michoacan state, when *campesinos* became so angered over the slaughter of their infected cattle that they attacked and stabbed to death 6 soldiers and a veterinarian who were making an inspection.

The commission's campaign ended Nov. 26 after the U.S., which carried the financial burden of the operation, had spent $20 million. The Commission declared the state of Tabasco entirely free of hoof-and-mouth disease Jan. 9, 1948.

New Bracero Accord

An updated farm labor agreement between Mexico and the U.S. was signed in Mexico City Aug. 2, 1951. The signing of the new treaty had been preceded by months of bitter controversy within the U.S over imported Mexican farm labor.

Mexico and the U.S. had participated since 1942 in a joint program for the employment in the U.S. of Mexican seasonal farm laborers. The laborers, known as *braceros,* had occasionally been a source of friction. Some Mexicans, known as "wetbacks," worked in the U.S. illegally. "Wetbacks" could not be protected by Mexico since their presence in the U.S. was not covered by the official *bracero* agreement, the Farm Labor Act of 1942. At the same time, their presence angered U.S. organized labor: they undercut the wages of U.S. farm laborers, and they tolerated work conditions that the U.S. labor movement had encouraged farm workers to reject.

U.S. immigration officials admitted by late 1950 that 30,000 Mexicans were stealing across the border into the U.S. every month and swelling agricultural unemployment rolls. The Immigration Service estimated that some 390,000 entered illegally during the 1950 fiscal year. 78,000 former "wetbacks" whose entry had been legalized were employed on U.S. farms in Dec. 1949. California Gov. Earl Warren guessed that his state alone had 44,000 illegally-resident Mexicans.

Deportation was expensive: U.S. immigration authorities arrested 579,000 "wetbacks" in 1950; it cost about $11 million to deport them.

A series of *N.Y, Times* articles Mar. 25-29, 1951 reported that: (1) more than 1,000,000 "wetbacks" entered the U.S. annually; (2) they worked under conditions "tantamount to peonage" for incredibly low wages (as low as 40 cents a day) and were supplied with the crudest housing or none at all; (3) by competing with U.S. labor, they depressed wage standards and working conditions and threw many U.S. farm hands out of work and on relief; (4) farmers from Texas to California reaped "fabulous" profits by merciless exploitation of "wetbacks."

U.S. legislators undertook to correct this situation in 1951. The upshot was the revision of the *bracero* program and the passing of a new U.S. farm labor bill July 12.

A U.S. Congressional controversy had preceded the enactment of the bill. The bill was initially passed by Senate voice vote May 7 and sent to the House. The measure proposed these penalties for employment of "wetbacks" by U.S. farmers: (1) up to $2,000 fine or imprisonment for up to one year for each alien so employed, (2) denial of legal Mexican laborers imported under the act to farmers who hired "wetbacks." Sen. Dennis Chavez (D.,N.M.) protested Apr. 27 and 30 that the pending measure would bring back peonage, benefit only big farmers and lower farm labor standards. The Mexicans were wanted by only 125,000 big farms owned by less than 2% of the nation's farm operators and producing only 7% of the nation's food and fiber. They offered employment only for an average of 90 days a year, he said.

Meantime U.S. federal officials May 1 began a "get-tough" policy of enforcing existing regulations against hiring "wetbacks."

The issue was brought to a head when members of a U.S. farm union, on strike against farm employers in California's Imperial Valley, accused farmers of using "wetbacks" as strikebreakers. H. L. Mitchell, president of the AFL (American Federation of Labor), National Farm Labor Union, charged May 27 that police and deputy sheriffs in the California towns of Brawley, Calexico and El Centro were rounding up "wetbacks" and escorting them through picket lines to be strikebreakers on Imperial Valley farms. 6,000 members of his union had gone on strike there May 24 in hopes of (1) forcing farmers to stop hiring Mexicans who enter the U.S. illegally, (2) gaining preferential hiring for American farm hands and (3) raising the 60-cent hourly pay. 19 members of the AFL National Farm Labor Union were reported arrested in Brawley, Calif. by June 4 for making "citizens' arrests" of wetbacks. 3 of them were sentenced June 3 on kidnaping charges. California law allowed citizens to arrest illegal immigrants and turn them over to the authorities. Union members had arrested about 1,200 suspected wetbacks so far. The Immigration Service began using planes to return them to Mexico June 1. (The Immigration Service reported Aug. 6 that 20,000 wetbacks—1/3 of those apprehended—had been flown back to Mexico in June and July.) Mexico's Foreign Ministry said June 2 that although legal contracting centers in Mexico were jammed with applicants, U.S. farmers preferred to hire wetbacks who worked for less than legal pay.

U.S. Labor Secy. Maurice J. Tobin June 8 ordered the removal of any Mexican contract workers found employed as strikebreakers on Imperial Valley farms. (The U.S.-Mexican agreement barred strikebreaking.) The striking National Farm Labor Union urged Pres. Truman June 11 to recall Amb.-to-Mexico William O'Dwyer. O'Dwyer's brother Frank was an Imperial Valley farmer and partner of keith Mets, president of the Valley Farmers Association.

Mexico informed the U.S. June 15 that contracting for Mexicans to work on U.S. farms would end June 30 when the U.S.-Mexican migratory labor agreement expired and that no Mexicans who had signed contracts would be allowed to leave Mexico for the U.S. after June 15. Mexico said it would extend the pact only on condition that the U.S. Congress provided penalties for American farmers who used wetbacks and arranged for all contracts to be signed by both governments. Mexico had already ordered its migratory workers to return home as soon as their U.S. contracts expired.

The National Farm Labor Union June 25 suspended until fall its picketing of Imperial Valley farms, where harvesting had ended. It accused the Labor Department of being "an employment agency for strikebreakers" for allegedly failing to remove contract Mexican laborers from struck farms.

The bill authorizing the Labor Department to recruit Mexicans for work on U.S. farms was passed in a new, compromise form by both houses of Congress and sent to Pres. Truman June 30. Joint conferees killed an amendment by Sen. Paul H. Douglas (D., Ill.) that would have imposed severe penalties on farmers hiring wetbacks. The measure set up improved standards of pay, tranportation and housing. Truman signed this new *bracero* bill July 12. He asked the U.S. Congress the next day for further legislation which would punish those who harbor wetbacks and permit federal agents to inspect farms without warrants. Organized U.S. labor had opposed the bill as too soft on farm employers, the President's request for additional provisions was designed to meet some of the labor criticism.

The enactment of the bill cleared the way for the new U.S.-Mexican agreement on the employment of Mexican *braceros* in the U.S. The Mexican-U.S. migrant labor treaty was signed in Mexico City Aug. 2.

Military Aid Rejected

As the Korean War (1950-3) neared its stalemated conclusion, anti-Communist pressures mounted in the U.S. The U.S. sought to enlist Mexico in an anti-Communist defense program by offering military aid in exchange for a Mexican commitment to cooperate in the the defence of so-called "democratic institutions." The move was seen as essentially an attempt to elicit support from Mexico in the "cold war." The Mexican government refused the offer.

The leading member of a U.S. military delegation to Mexico City, Maj. Gen. Edward M. Jones, returned to Washington Feb. 21, 1952 after 2 weeks of futile negotiations. The purpose of the talks had been to draft an accord for the extension of U.S. military aid supplier to Mexico. The U.S. delegation had pointed out to its Mexican counterpart that the U.S. Mutual Security Act required that all countries receiving American military aid subscribe to "the defense of democracy" throughout the world. The Mexican delegation interpreted this requirement to mean that Mexico might be held responsible for sending troops outside national territory in the event of a Latin-American conflict. This contradicted the much-cherished Mexican principle of non-intervention, a fundamental belief inherited from the Revolution. Accordingly, the Mexican delegation refused to accept the offer of U.S. military aid unless all such defense obligations were withdrawn. This decision was rejected by the U.S. delegation as unacceptable. The Mexican government's position was backed by all Mexican political parties, especially the parties of the left.

The Mexico City correspondent of the *N.Y. Times* commented Feb. 21: "Anti-American feeling is still strong throughout the populace, and the left has a considerable hold on public opinion. Rightly or wrongly, the government feels that it cannot go against this sentiment, particularly in an election year. The failure of the negotiations was an important success for the Mexican Communist Party and its left-wing allies. They have been conducting a vigorous and vocal campaign against any defense agreement with the United States, and their victory is bound to win them further prestige."

NEW ECONOMIC & POLITICAL STABILITY

It was widely agreed that Mexico's new postwar stability was strengthened during the term of Miguel Aleman. The U.S. played a major role in the increasing social and economic calm by underwriting a bilaterally negotiated parity between the Mexican peso and the U.S. dollar. The PRI-dominated Mexican government and the U.S. became friendlier than ever before, while the Mexican government began a crackdown on extremist domestic opposition groups.

U.S. Helps Stabilize Peso

Mexico reduced the foreign exchange value of the peso July 22, 1948, largely in hopes of attracting more tourists and foreign sales. The peso had been pegged at 4.85 to the U.S. dollar since 1940. The new temporary rate July 23 was 5.75-6 pesos to $1.

In an official statement, an Economy Ministry spokesman said July 22 that: (1) The Bank of Mexico's dollar, gold and silver reserves had fallen to U.S. $114 million during the past week; (2) Mexico had already drawn U.S.$37 million (of the U.S. $50 million available to it under a currency stabilization credit arranged with the U.S. in 1947) in an effort to prevent devalution; (3) the devaluation of the peso would not affect policy with regard to the government's foreign debt.

The spokesman set forth the following pro-devaluation arguments: (1) The lower exchange rate would benefit Mexico's tourism industry by attracting U.S. and other tourists; (2) Since Mexico was an exporting country (primarily of metals), the devaluation would increase the market abroad for Mexican goods. It was revealed Aug. 2 that the dollar drain had exceeded U.S. $19.5 million in July, as compared with less than U.S.$5 million in June.

Mexico Aug. 12 fixed retail prices of rice, flour, lard, beans and salt to curb rising living costs.

Aleman, in his 2d annual report to Congress promised Sept. 1 to push his industrial expansion and anti-inflation programs and defended the devaluation, which had provoked strong political attacks on his administration.

The Mexican government June, 1, 1949 again announced a new official exchange rate for the peso—7.85 to the dollar. The previous rate was 6.85. The new rate was applicable only for import and export tax conversions. The devaluation was undertaken after the peso had hit a new low of 8.40 May 20, 1949.

The Bank of Mexico also disclosed a plan for offering an unlimited amount of silver coins to the international market. Samples of these coins (minted in Mexico, one of the world's greatest silver producers) about the size of the U.S. silver dollar and weighing one troy ounce with 0.925 fineness had been flown to banks and governments throughout the world. The plan would turn Mexico into the world's leading silver clearing house and help build up the depleted foreign reserves largely resposible for the low stability of the peso. Mexican officials expressed hope that Mexico would eventually create its own exchange for the coins.

Mexico City and Washington D.C. announced June 18, 1949 the stabilization of the peso at a new parity of 8.65 pesos to the dollar. At the same time U.S. Treasury Secy. John W. Snyder announced a new Mexican-American currency stabilization agreement supplementing the 1947 stabilization pact under which the U.S. fund for the stabilization of the peso would be increased by $25 million.

The Mexican government June. 21, 1949 barred 206 "unessential" imports, most of them from the U.S. In a related move the government slashed most export tarriffs by 80% July 5.

Alemán told the new Chamber of Deputies in his annual "state of the nation" address Sept. 1, 1949 that devaluation of the peso had saved Mexico from an inflationary and foreign trade crisis. He promised to retain government controls over prices and distribution of consumer goods. He also disclosed that the Bank of America had granted a $3 million loan for the construction of a transoceanic highway across the Isthmus of Tehuantepec.

Foreign Firm Indemnified, Other Oil Developments

Pres. Aleman announced Sept. 1, 1949, in a message to Congress, that agreement had been reached on a settlement of the Mexican Eagle Oil Co.'s compensation claims for the nationalization of its properties in Mexico in 1938. Mexico would pay the company an indemnity of $81¼ million plus 3%

interest from Mar. 18, 1938 to Sept. 18, 1948. The company was controlled jointly by the Royal Dutch Co. and the Shell Transport & Trading Co. Mexican Eagle Oil's issued capital had exceeded $59 million in Aug. 1949.

Mexico Nov. 24 announced the discovery of a rich new oil field (Tortugero) near the Gulf port of Coatzacoalcos.

Among other developments in the field of oil extraction during the Aleman administration: (1) A $30 million Texas Co. loan to Pemex, the government oil monopoly, was announced June 25, 1948, in Mexico City. (2) Pemex signed a 12-year drilling contract with a U.S. group headed by Edwin W. Pauley in Mexico City Mar. 5, 1949; under the agreement, the American group, a new company named Mexican American Independent, would receive 15% of the value of the production of the wells it drilled but exploitation would be carried out by Pemex. (3) A new oil refinery was opened Dec. 26, 1950, at Reynosa on the Texas border. (4) Pemex bought the Mexican Gulf Oil Co. and subsidiaries in Mexico for $2.35 million Jan. 18, 1951. (5) New oil discoveries in 1951 raised Mexico's known oil reserves to 1.37 billion barrels. (6) The last dispute remaining from Mexico's 1938 oil expropriation was settled Sept. 4 when the Mexican government bought the Charro Oil Co. for $1,852,000. Charro was formerly owned by Sinclair (U.S.).

Economic Stability

The Mexican economy was described as relatively stable by 1951. Major factors in this new stability were the continuing U.S.-Mexican agreement on the peso and the influx of U.S. dollars into Mexico since the start of the Korean War. U.S. companies, *braceros* working in the U.S. and European World War II refugees bringing newly unfrozen capital into the country were the main sources of the dollars.

Mexico's dollar reserves, down to $200 million in 1948, had climbed to $344 million (as compared with the World War II peak of $355 million), Treasury Min. Ramon Beteta reported Mar. 10. The financial condition "has improved so much in 12 months," he said, "that we won't ask for any more" U.S. loans. Mexico nevertheless received U.S. Export-Import Bank credits totaling $56 million Aug. 12 for railway projects.

In order to cut down dollar circulation the government Jan. 12 had ordered that future increases in private bank deposits of dollars be turned over to the Bank of Mexico. Restrictions on imports also were lifted.

Mexico reduced export taxes July 23 by 50% to 83% on many major products, including shrimp, fish, cocoa beans, vanilla, tobacco, citrus fruits, cotton textiles and silver jewelry. The tax cuts served to keep export prices down by offsetting a rise in production costs.

Mexico and the U.S. agreed July 27 to continue their pact on stabilization of the Mexican peso until 1953. The U.S. Monetary Stabilization Fund announced a plan to buy up to 50 million pesos ($5,870,000) to keep the peso pegged at 8.65 to $1 until 1953.

Mexico's foreign trade showed a $125 million deficit in 1951, but this was offset by a "considerable improvement" in the country's monetary reserves, the Bank of Mexico reported Feb. 1, 1952.

Pres. Aleman Dec. 11, 1951 had announced a balanced 1952 budget, the highest in Mexican history. It called for expenditures of nearly 4 billion pesos ($464 million) and showed a surplus of 2,150,000 pesos.

The Mexican government announced Jan. 14, 1952 that it would try to develop iron deposits in the Las Truchas district on the Pacific coast without foreign aid. The deposits had been owned by the Bethlehem Steel Co. before they were expropriated.

Private U.S. mining interests expressed disappointment Jan. 29, 1952 over government regulations setting up restrictions on uranium and other fissionable ore mining. The U.S. government had hoped for a speedup in research in this field.

The government Jan. 30 banned the export of certain essential commodities (only sugar and rice were named;

cotton was exempted) until domestic production curbed price rises.

Mexico reduced its export tariffs on many products July 19 to increase sales abroad by lowering prices. Included in the tariff cut were frozen shrimp, fish, honey, shark livers, flowers, cocoa, onions, garlic, citrus fruits, cotton textiles and partially manufactured forms of lead and zinc.

The government announced May 30, 1952 the approval by the U.S. Export-Import Bank of 2 new loans, part of a $150 million credit opened in 1951. $4 million was spent to finish the Oviachic irrigation dam, $1½ million for new telegraph and phone facilities.

Opposition Forces Curbed

The Aleman administration cracked down on several persistent opposition elements:

(1) The Sinarquist Union, a right-wing, nationalist and proclerical political party, was banned by the Mexican government Jan. 28, 1949. The Department of the Interior described the union as "undemocratic, seditious, and a threat to public order," and "in open conflict with democratic institutions." The union was further accused of maintaining relations with the Falange of Spain (Mexico did not recognize Francisco Franco's Spain and still accepted the accreditation of a Spanish Republican mission in Mexico City) and of subordination to the Catholic Church (Catholic political groups were technically illegal in Mexico because of a built-in anticlerical clause in the constitution forbidding "subordination to an international organization"). The Sinarquistas were often openly referred to as "Fascist."

These postwar events had led to the banning of the Sinarquistas: After the 1946 elections the Sinarquistas began to set up an opposition party, the Popular Force (Fuerza Popular), in an attempt to gain power through parliamentary means. The Popular Force was legally established June 9, 1948, and the party platform was published in a pamphlet called Mexico 1960. The Sinarquistas were able to win several state and municipal offices, especially in Leon (Guanajuato state). To symbolize their rejection of the anti-clerical constitution, the *Sinarquistas* had draped in black shrouds the statue of Benito Juarez (a great 19th-century revolutionary hero) on the Alameda in Mexico City. The government retaliated by denying registration to the party and then outlawing it.

(2) Mexico's Interior Ministry Sept. 13, 1951 rejected an application from the Mexican Communist party (PCM) for recognition as a political party entitled to enter slates in the next state and national elections. The Interior Ministry claimed that with fewer than 30,000 members the PCM was ineligible for recognition. (The ministry was investigating charges that the PCM had infiltrated the leadership of striking northern coal miners and encouraged their intransigeance during a Mar. 1949 labor dispute.) The PCM in return accused the government of "submitting to orders from Washington." PCM Secy. Gen. Dionisio Encina was arrested for leading a demonstration against Aleman in Mexico City Sept. 1.

(3) Marxist labor chief Vicente Lombardo Toledano was expelled Jan. 7, 1948, from the biggest government labor union, the CTM *(Confederación de Trabajadores Mexicanos, Federation of Mexican Workers)* despite the fact that Lombardo Toledano had been the principal founder of the PRI-affiliated trade and craft union. He had formed the CTM in 1936 with the backing of Mexico's populist Pres. Lazaro Cárdenas (served 1934-40). Lombardo Toledano, however, had run afoul of Cárdenas' successor, Manuel Avila Camacho (served 1940-46), and his prestige in the CTM slipped drastically during World War II when Camacho for a time removed him from the CTM's leadership.

It was widely believed that Lombardo Toledano had been expelled from the CTM for associating with Soviet Amb-to-Mexico Constantine Oumanski. Oumanski was accused by many government officials of heading a subversive ring in Mexico City.

Lombardo Toledano reacted to his expulsion by organizing his own political party, the *Partido Popular* (PP). The

Partido Popular (later *Partido Popular Socialista,* PPS) challenged the ruling PRI in the 1949 general elections to the Mexican Chamber of Deputies (Mexican congressional elections are held every 3 years).

The elections took place July 3, 1949. The *Partido Popular* placed a very weak 3d in the vote, following the PRI and PAN *(Partido de Accion Nacional);* PAN was an opposition party of Catholic conservatives sympathetic to but not as extremist as the *Sinarquistas;* it demanded an end to official government anticlericalism. The PRI won 142 seats, the PAN 4 seats, the *Partido Popular* only 1 seat. (There were 2,991,992 registered voters—women did not yet have the right to vote in congressional elections.)

Controversy surrounded Lombardo Toledano again in 1949 when a Continental Congress for Peace opened in Mexico Sept. 5 with 1,000 leftist and pacifist delegates attending from Western Hemisphere countries. Leaders of the conference denied that it was directed from Moscow, but only one speaker during the first 6 days criticized the Soviet Union. Lombardo Toledano, who was the Mexican leader of the conference, said Sept. 6 that "the forces of peace" must be "effectively organized [in] every factory, laboratory, office and school." He denied Mexican press charges that he was trying to revive the Comintern (Moscow-sponsored Communist international revolutionary organization), by disguising it as a league of pacifists. Lombardo Toledano's old friend ex-Pres. Lazaro Cardenas, in a letter of encouragement to the conference, deplored the formation of regional blocs "outside the framework of the UN" before World War II was liquidated by the completion of major peace treaties.

Lombardo Toledano's *Partido Popular* remained in existence in opposition to the government despite its poor showing in the 1949 elections. It nominated Lombardo Toledano as presidential candidate Dec. 15, 1951 and ran him unsuccessfully against Adolfo Ruiz Cortines in the July 6, 1952 presidential elections.

RUIZ CORTINES ADMINISTRATION, 1952-8

Although he was Miguel Aleman's protege, when Adolfo Ruiz Cortines became president he eliminated much of the corruption and graft that had pervaded the federal government during Aleman's administration.

Ruiz Cortines' most strikingly independent act against corruption was the government seizure of 10,000 acres of farmland in Tampico owned by 4 friends of Aleman's. The land, which the government claimed had been obtained through graft, belonged to ex-Agriculture Min. Nazario Ortíz Garza, ex-Sen. Carlos I. Serrano (one of Alemán's closest henchman), ex-Economy Min. and Amb -to-Italy Ramón Beteta and Carlos S. Oriani. Ruiz Cortines also cancelled a major oil distribution monopoly granted by Alemán to his personal friend Jorge Pasquel, an industrialist.

Ruiz Cortines was born in Veracruz in 1890 of a poor family. During the revolution he worked first for Madero and then for Carranza. He was elected to the Chamber of Deputies in 1937. An early friend of Aleman's, he served as governor of Veracruz state and as Aleman's minister of the interior *(Secretario de gobernacion)*. Like many interior Ministers (including Aleman), Ruiz Cortines was groomed for the presidency while he held the interior portfolio.

Ruiz Cortines Elected President

Adolfo Ruiz Cortines, 61, candidate of the ruling PRI *(Partido Revolucionario Institucional)*, was elected July 6, 1952 by one of the largest votes to date to succeed Miguel Alemán as president for a 6-year term beginning Dec. 1.

Official returns gave Ruiz Cortines 2,713,419 out of nearly 5 million votes cast. Efrain Gonzales Luna, candidate of the Catholic right-wing PAN *(Partido de Accion Nacional)*, polled 285,555 votes, Gen. Miguel Henriquez Guzman of a loose new left-oriented coalition, the Federated People's Party polled 579,745 votes, and Vicente Lombardo Toledano of the leftist *Partido Popular* polled 72,482 votes.

The supporters of Gen. Henriquez Guzman, known as *Henriquistas,* were urging a return to the extreme populist policies of the Cardenas era. A post-election clash between Mexico City police and *Henriquistas* July 7 climaxed what had been regarded until then as Mexico's most orderly election. Henriquistas charged July 9 that the government "kidnapped" bodies of a "considerable number" of persons killed in the 4-hour fight, but Mexico City officials said July 8 that no fatalities had occurred. Pro-Henriques Gen. Candido Aguilar of the Revolutionary Party and Ignacio Ramos Praslow of the Constitutionalist Party were arrested July 8; they denied July 9 they planned to incite armed revolt. Outgoing Pres. *Aleman granted amnesty* Aug. 26 to 128 persons, including Aguilar and Ramos Praslow, arrested in the post-election riots.

Henriquez Guzmán accused the government again Oct. 4 of trying to create "a state of alarm" by "kidnaping" some of his followers. 5 *Henriquista* leaders had been arrested Oct. 2 and released the same day after questioning. Congress had condemned Henriquez' post-election political activities as "subversive." The resolution condemning Henriquez was adopted Oct. 2 after Henriquez had pointedly told newspapermen he was "at the will of the people" and would "do what the people order."

Ruiz Cortines was inaugurated as president of Mexico Dec. 1 in Mexico City. He promised anti-corruption and anti-profiteering campaigns and a good-neighbor policy in foreign relations as the basis of his administration. He added "freedom to criticize the government" to a list of guaranteed freedoms: thought, press, religion and economic and spiritual liberty.

Ruiz Cortines named a cabinet with these members: *Interior*—Angel Carzajal; *Foreign Affairs*—Luis Padilla Nervo; *Finance*—Antonio Carrillo Flores; *Defense*—Gen. Matias Ramos; *Agriculture*—Gilberio Flores Munoz; *Communications* —Carlos Lazo; *Economy*—Gilberto Loyo; *Education*—Jose

Angel Ceniceros; *Health*—Ignacio Morones Prieto; *Navy*—Gen. Rodolfo Sanchez Taboada; *Labor*—Adolfo Lopez Mateos; *Hydraulic Resources*—Eduardo Chavez; *National Resources*—Jose Lopez Lira; *Governor of the Federal District*—Ernesto Uruchurtu.

Other leading officials: *Agrarian Department*—Castulo Villasenor; *Attorney General*—Carlos Franco Sodi; *Att. General for Districts & Territories*—Guillermo Aguilar y Maya; *Presidential Secretary*—Enrique Codriguez Cano; *Private Secretary*—Salvador Olmos.

U.S. Vice Pres.-elect Richard M. Nixon, personal representative of U.S. Pres.-elect Dwight D. Eisenhower at the inauguration, told a joint session of the Mexican Congress Dec. 3 that a major objective of the incoming U.S. Republican administration would be to develop "most friendly relations" between the U.S. and other American republics.

(In an act seen as an historic symbol of reconciliation and a gesture of accommodation with the Catholic opposition, retiring, Pres. Aleman publicly embraced Archbishop Luis Maria Martinez Nov. 26 in the Basilica of Guadalupe, Mexico's national shrine. Alemán unveiled a plaque in the shrine as one of his last official acts.)

DOMESTIC POLITICS

The 6 years of the Ruiz Cortines administration constituted one of Mexico's most peaceful periods. The absence of marked social discord was attributed by many observers largely to the respect that Ruiz Cortines commanded. Even when Aleman served in Ruiz Cortines cabinet, Ruiz Cortines appeared to be thoroughgoing in his attempt to uproot the government corruption that had set in during the Aleman's presidential term.

The opposition to the PRI, which had won more than 25% ef the vote in the 1952 presidential elections, dissipated during the Ruiz Cortines era. Veteran leftist Vicente Lombardo Toledano, an implacable foe of Aleman's, agreed to support Ruiz Cortines soon after the latter's election. But

the *Henriquistas* and the Communists, who were more intransi-
geant, were sharply repressed in the early years of the new
administration; the government treated them as a subversive
rather than a loyal opposition.

PRI Curbs Opposition

The total opposition vote against the PRI in the 1952
elections had for the first time represented the possibility of a
real threat to PRI supremacy. Following the election, the
government moved to eliminate the major opposition groups
through either reconciliation or outright legal curbs.

Marxist ex-labor leader Lombardo Toledano had opposed
the ruling PRI during the 1952 campaign on the grounds
that it was not ideologically militant enough. Lombardo
Toledano had initially tried to make common cause with
other opposition candidates, but negotiations had broken
down over his insistence that nationalization of banks,
phones, electricity and other major industries be made an
opposition coalition plank. Lombardo Toledano eventually
ran independently on the *Partido Popular* ticket. The Mexico
City pro-government press alleged after the election Dec.
30-1 that Lombardo Toledano, had written to Communist
Chinese Pres. Mao Tse-tung Sept. 2, praising the "high
ideals" for which Communist China was fighting in Korea
and campaigning throughout the Far East. Lombardo
Toledano charged Jan. 2, 1953 that photostats of the pur-
ported latter to Mao exhibited by Mexico City newspapers had
been "fabricated" by political followers of ex-Pres. Miguel
Aleman.

Despite this controversy, Lombardo Toledano met with
Ruiz Cortines for informal reconciliation talks Dec. 18, 1952.
Lombardo Toledano declared his support for Ruiz Cortines
Jan. 29, 1953 and urged his *Partido Popular* to support the
new administration. Lombardo Toledano said that "we have
not changed" but that Ruiz Cortines had in effect adopted
the opposition program, "so now we can honestly say the
opposition won the election."

In an implicitly anti-Communist move, the Mexican Congress Dec. 31, 1953 passed legislation requiring a political party to have a membership of at least 75,000 to take part in national elections. Total Communist party membership was estimated at under half that figure.

The government Feb. 2, 1954, banned the Federated People's Party (the biggest opposition to the PRI but a weak 2d in the 1952 elections) from entering candidates in federal elections. The party led by Gen. Miguel Henriquez Guzman, was accused of subversive activity in its opposition to the Ruiz Cortines regime.

Women Vote

Mexican women July 4, 1955 voted for the first time in a Congressional election. (Mexican Congressional elections are held once every 3 years.) The PRI won by a large majority in the election.

A constitutional amendment allowing women to vote in presidential elections had been approved by a majority of the 28 state legislatures Mar. 11, 1953. It was approved by Congress and became law Dec. 31, 1954. An extension of the total franchise to women had long been a major plan of the PRI and had been among Ruiz Cortines campaign promises.

Strikes & Civil Disturbances in Mexico City

Mexico City was battered by labor and student violence in 1958, Ruiz Cortines' last year in office.

There were 2 major strikes: (1) State telegraph workers struck Feb. 5, and rejected Feb. 15 a 12% wage increase offered by Ruiz Cortines. The strike was solved through Ruiz Cortines mediation toward the end of the month. More than 7,000 workers had demanded a full 50% increase over their previous average pay of $52 a month. (2) A 5-day rail strike with daily work stoppages ended June 30 after Ruiz Cortines agreed to study workers' demands for a 250 peso ($20)

monthly raise, nearly 50% higher than their previous wage.
The dispute was ended through mediation.

Rioting students seized buses in Mexico City Aug. 23
in protest against a fare rise that took effect Aug. 19. Some
of the vehicles were hidden within University City, an autonomous organization barred to police. Federal police reclaim-
ed 80 buses late Aug. 23, but they rioters claimed they still
held 145. An estimated 100 persons were injured in clashes
between drivers and students and in accidents involving stu-
dent-driven buses.

Riots also were staged Aug. 28-30 by wildcat groups
in the union of Pemex (nationalized petroleum industry)
workers. Police opened fire on demonstrators who refused
to disperse in the face of water hoses and tear gas. Dissident
union workers at Pemex, who had staged a hunger strike in
front of the main employes' entrance, were forcibly removed
Aug. 28 by federal police.

More rioting took place in Mexico City Sept. 6 this
time over an official ban on a rally by dissident members of
a gradeschool teachers' union. The riot caused injuries to
300 persons. Truckloads of federal police, using tear gas and
truncheons, clashed with the demonstrators and succeeded in
preventing the mass rally by leftist members of the National
Educational Workers Union. Othon Salazar Ramirez, leader
of the union's leftist faction, and several of his aides were
arrested.

In his final address to the nation Sept. 1, retiring Pres.
Ruiz Cortines charged that groups "foreign to the national
interest" were inciting laborers "to abandon their responsible
conduct." He said that recent labor violence had placed the
nation in grave danger. A roundup of known Communists
by Interior Ministry agents resulted in the arrest of 40 persons,
8 of them citizens or one-time residents of the U.S., it
was reported Sept. 10. 3 of the Americans were deported
Sept. 8-9. The ministry said it had proof that Communist
agitators had given money and other assistance in the
recent wave of strikes among railway workers, students and
teachers.

RELATIONS WITH U.S.

Ruiz Cortines policy toward the U.S. was essentially a prolongation of the "Good Neighbor" relationship, which had characterized the Camacho (1940-6) and Aleman (1946-52) administrations.

The U.S. continued to provide development credits and loans to Mexico, and the U.S.-Mexican agreement on migrant workers was extended. Ruiz Cortines' term, which was roughly contemporaneous with Dwight D. Eisenhower's Republican administration in the U.S. (1953-60), was marked by tranquillity in U.S.-Mexican relations and by the gradual decline of the "wetback" problem.

A Mexican-American joint irrigation and hydroelectric project on the Rio Grande river was inaugurated Oct. 19, 1953 by the presidents of the 2 nations, Ruíz Cortines and Dwight D. Eisenhower. The dam was projected under a 1944 river treaty between the 2 countries for the dual purpose of water-control and the generation of electricity. The project, called the Falcon Dam, was located on the Rio Grande between Laredo and Rio Grande City, about 200 miles from the mouth of the river at the Gulf of Mexico. It had been estimated that 726,000 million gallons of water had been "wasted" annually in the lower Rio Grande. Mexicans had also suffered from both floods and droughts in the area.

Ruiz Cortines conferred with U.S. Pres. Eisenhower Mar. 26-28, 1956 at the Greenbrier Hotel at White Sulphur Springs, W. Va. Eisenhower Feb. 23 had invited Ruiz Cortines and Canadian Prime Min. Louis Stephen St. Laurent to meet with him. White House Press Secy. James C. Hagerty said Eisenhower wanted "the heads of government of these neighboring North American countries to know each other better and to discuss informally matters of common interest." Following the agendaless 3-day meeting, all participants indicated that the talks had been valuable and that they thought similar meetings should be held in the future.

Minor irritants to Mexican-American friendship during this period were the shrimp-boat controversy and the debate over the ownership of Mexican border land by U.S. citizens. Mexico disputed the right of U.S.-owned shrimp boats to fish in waters off the Mexican coast and to use Mexican ports to put in for refueling or during bad weather. The issue was never satisfactorily solved because of the refusal of a substantial minority of U.S. shrimp boats to cooperate with proposed bilateral agreements. U.S. ownership of Mexican border land was ended by government decree, however. The expropriation decree was signed July 31, 1958, by Ruiz Cortines; it stated that no foreigner might own real estate within 100 kilometers of the border or 50 kilometers of the coast. A compensation value was to be fixed on all expropriated properties after appraisal and the sum was to be put in escrow until the claimants agreed on its apportionment. The largest affected property was the 648,853-acre Cananea ranch, owned by U.S. citizens. It was expropriated Aug. 20, 1958.

During Ruiz Cortines term, the U.S. made a major financial contribution toward railway construction in Mexico. Among the largest loans were a $61 million loan in 1954 for new railways and a $28.6 credit in 1958 to the National Railways of Mexico for purchases of U.S. locomotives, rolling stock, communications and track equipment.

Bracero Program Extended

The U.S.' Farm Labor Act, a law under which Mexican seasonal farm laborers *(braceros)* were allowed to work in the U.S. in the event of labor shortages, came up for renewal several times during the Ruiz Cortines administration.

Mexico favored the continuation of the U.S. farm labor program, which eased the Mexican "underemployment" problem. (Like many agricultural nations Mexico had widespread temporary unemployment, known as "under-employment," following harvest periods.) The Mexican Labor Ministry insisted on welfare provisions for the *braceros,* however, as well as pay parity with U.S. citizens engaged in farm work.

The continuation of the program was supported in the U.S. by farmers in need of labor help during seasonal shortages.

But the U.S. labor movement, especially the AFL-affiliated Farm Labor Union, was critical of the program as it had been run previously. A major bone of contention the illegal immigrant workers, or "wetbacks." U.S. labor contended that "wetbacks" were a manpower reserve that could be used by farm employers to glut the farm labor market and force down wages.

The latest U.S.-Mexican farm-labor program (signed Aug. 2, 1951, before the Ruiz Cortines administration) expired Jan. 15, 1954.

A bill for continued recruitment of Mexican laborers for work on U.S. farms, with or without Mexican government consent, was passed by U.S. House voice vote Mar. 2 and by a 59-52 Senate vote Mar. 3, 1954. The program's bilateral renewal had beed stalled by the U.S.' refusal to grant Mexican demands for welfare guarantees to the migrants. Southwestern farmers had demanded the right to recruit Mexican border-jumpers if necessary to ease a regional labor shortage.

Pres. Eisenhower Mar. 16 signed the bill, which permitted Mexican farm laborers to enter the U.S. through Dec. 31, 1955. It provided that the workers would be recruited at 6 Mexican border stations and paid not less than the prevailing wage received by Americans.

Meanwhile, Mexico and the U.S. Mar. 10, 1954 signed a 2-year extension of the labor recruitment pact, which had expired Jan. 15. These were the major changes: border recruiting was permitted; Mexicans who quit before their contracts expired would have to pay part of their return fare: and employers were required to offer on-the-job insurance, as well as occupational insurance, at the workers'e xpense. (The U.S.-Mexican agreement on the employment of Mexican farm laborers in the U.S., due to expire Dec. 31, was extended through 1956 under an another agreement reached Dec. 23, 1954.)

Earl M. Hugher, administrator of the U.S. Agriculture Department's Commodity Stabilization Service, urged at a House Agriculture subcommittee hearing Mar. 16, 1955 that the program for importing Mexican farm laborers be made permanent without change. But Asst. Labor Secy. Rocco C. Siciliano urged a limited $4\frac{1}{2}$-year extension with such changes

as: (a) a requirement that U.S. workers be offered transportation, housing and insurance comparable to those of imported workers; (b) a provision making it clear that U.S. farmers
could not pay Mexicans less than U.S. workers.

Largely as a consequence of demands by U.S. labor, the
new version of the program was supplemented by a drive
("Operation Wetback") against Mexican nationals working
illegally in the U.S. The *N.Y. Herald Tribune* reported Dec.
21, 1954 that there was "a substantial increase this year" in
the hiring of *braceros* on U.S. farms, apparently as a result
of steps by U.S. authorities to halt the influx of wetbacks.
U.S. Immigration Commissioner Joseph M. Swing reported
July 29, 1954 that the Border Patrol had seized 52,374 wetbacks in the California-western Arizona area June 17-July 27
and 44,403 in southern Texas June 15-July 27. 45,953 others
returned voluntarily from Texas to Mexico, and 10,917 were
seized at California-Arizona roadblocks prior to the drive
against the illegal immigrants. Swing asserted July 20, 1955
that Operation Wetback, completed in 1954, had "paid off by
reducing illegal entries . . . by more than 86.4%." Swing said
arrests of illegally entered Mexicans averaged) 3,000 a day
before Operation Wetback but had declined during the past
6 months to an average of 350 a day "despite the fact that
it is [currently] the height of the Texas cotton picking
season." Operation Wetback "brought effective control of
the southeast border [against illegal entry of Mexican farm
workers] for the first time," Swing declared in a 1955 year-
end report. Arrests of wetbacks by border patrolmen declined
from more than 640,000 in 1954 to fewer than 105,000 in
1955, Swing said. 450,000 legal agricultural workers (largely
braceros from Mexico) were imported during 1956.

OTHER DEVELOPMENTS

Peso Devalued Again

Mexico devalued its currency (with International Monetary Fund approval) Apr. 17, 1954. The new devaluation, the

latest in a series of devaluations instituted during the Aleman administration, made the U.S. dollar worth 12½ instead of 8.65 pesos. The government said the move was designed to increase exports, attract foreign investments, curtail imports and end a run on the peso.

Retail prices of non-rationed imported goods rose 30% to 40% after the devaluation, and food prices soared. The government started emergency sales of essential foods at controlled rates in Mexico City Apr. 22 in an effort to hold down prices.

The government reported a significant rise in gold and dollar reserves in the period following the devaluation. Pres. Adolfo Ruiz Cortines said Sept. 1, 1955, in his annual message to Congress, that the country had enjoyed a record high level of economic activity the previous 12 months, with the gold and dollar reserve increasing to $305 million as against $169 million Aug. 30, 1954.

Mexico's monetary agreement with the U.S. on stabilization of the peso was extended through 1957 under terms adopted Dec. 2, 1955. The U.S. made $75 million available for the new 2-year period.

Natural Disasters

Mexico was hit severely by natural disasters in 1954. This was particularly crippling in a nation in which more than half of the labor force worked in agriculture pursuits.

An earthquake inflicted extensive damage Feb. 5 on the villages of Petalcingo, Yajalon, Chilon and Tila in southern Mexico. At least 4 persons were reported killed by landslides.

The Rio Grande river valley June 27-28 suffered the worst floods in the river's history. The Mexican town of Piedras Negras was partially destroyed and about half the population of 35,000 made homeless. More than 150 persons were reported killed though only 38 bodies were recovered. Downstream the flood was adequately held by the newly built Falcon Dam.

Hurricane Janet and accompanying rains and floods caused more than 500 deaths in the Caribbean area and Mexico by Oct. 5 and left more than 100,000 Mexicans homeless. More than 200 were reported killed in the leveling of Chetumal, capital of Quintana Roo territory on the Yucatan Peninsula, which was hit Sept. 28. The Yucatan towns of Xcalak, Sacxan and Bacalar also were destroyed. Further north, on Mexico's gulf coast, 75% of Tampico was reported under water by Oct. 4, and 60,000 of the 114,000 inhabitants found themselves without homes. Thousands of squares miles in the vicinity were flooded. Hundreds of people were reported clinging to roofs and dikes or marooned on hills. Many were rescued by helicopters from the U.S. carrier *Saipan,* which arrived from Pensacola, Fla. Oct. 1 with food, medicine and doctors. Rough waters made it difficult for small rescue boats to operate. Many refugees were stricken by disease. 5 men were killed Sept. 30 in the crash of a Mexican relief plane en route from Merida to Chetumal.

Diego Rivera Dies

Diego Rivera, 70, the Mexican muralist, died Nov. 24, 1958 in Mexico City of a heart attack. He had attracted world attention in the 1930s for his leading role in the "Mexican School" of painting. The movement, which produced both mural and easel paintings and counted among others Jose Clemente Orozco, David Alfaro Siqueiros and Rufino Tamayo, was noted for its monumental pictures and harsh depiction of social injustice.

As a cultural figure of international stature, Rivera often did not hesitate to draw press attention to his involvement with social causes. Rivera was a supporter of various forms of international communism, and his mural in the RCA Building in New York was destroyed because he refused to delete from it a portrait of Bolshevik leader Lenin. He was twice expelled from the Mexican Communist Party for alleged sympathy with the 4th (Trotskyite) International. (Rivera had known Trotsky before the latter's assasination in Mexico

City in 1940.)

The Aleman administration Mar. 18, 1952 had returned to Rivera a controversial mural he had painted for a government-sponsored art exhibition in Paris. The government had rejected the mural because of its pro-Communist, anti-U.S. theme and held it for "safekeeping" for several days. It was given to the artist when he returned an advance payment of 10,000 pesos. The mural, *Nightmare of War and Dream of Peace,* depicts a saintly Stalin and Mao Tse-tung offering a peace pact to Westerners, one of whom is a villainous Uncle Sam. Rivera charged that the painting was rejected because of "pressure of North American imperialists."

But Rivera announced in Mexico City Apr. 14, 1956, that he was a Catholic. Rivera's disclosure came after he appeared at the Del Prado Hotel to paint out the words *"Dios no existe"* (God doesn't exist) from his mural *Sunday in the Alameda.* The painting had been hanging covered since 1948.

LOPEZ MATEOS ADMINISTRATION, 1958-64

The problems facing Mexico during the administration of Adolfo Lopez Mateos were considered for the most part to have been inherited from the Aleman and Ruiz Cortines periods. Many observers held that Lopez Mateos intelligently handled the fundamental issue of reconciling continued government sponsorship of the populist-type social program inherited from the Revolution with the need for more capitalization and industrial development.

A major new issue, however, was the birth of a revolutionary regime in nearby Cuba. The Lopez Mateos administration followed a policy of neutrality in the U.S.-Cuba dispute: Fortunately for Mexico, the Mexican government was never compelled to choose sides. Yet during the "Cuban missile crisis" of 1962, in which not only hemispheric but also world peace was seen as imperiled, the Mexican government leaned gently toward the U.S. by expressing its concern to Cuba over its harboring of Soviet offensive weapons.

Lopez Mateos was born in 1910, the year of the uprising against Porfirio Diaz. He grew up in Mexico City and, on finishing secondary school, became a history and literature teacher at the Normal Institute of Toluca (Mexico state). He earned his law degree by taking night courses and became involved in Toluca's Socialist politics. He joined the PRN (*Partido Nacional de la Revolucion,* predecessor of the PRI) in 1929.

As a reward for campaigning for Aleman, Lopez Mateos was nominated PRI candidate for Mexico state senator in 1946. Later in the Aleman administration, Lopez Mateos was appointed ambassador to Costa Rica.

Ruiz Cortines chose Lopez Mateos as his campaign manager in 1952. During the Ruiz Cortines administration Lopez Mateos held the post of labor minister and won party acclaim for his skill as a labor mediator. Only 13 of the labor disputes that arose then developed into strikes, all of which were handled by the Labor Ministry. Lopez Mateos was also in charge of negotiating with the U.S. over the *bracero* issue. During his own presidential campaign, he stressed the need for development of the backward and neglected rural sections of Mexico; he also promised to broaden Mexico's international role. Lopez Mateos did in fact sponsor a major agrarian reform beginning in Aug. 1962; he also toured Europe and received visits from many heads of state including John F. Kennedy, Charles de Gaulle, Tito, Jawaharlal Nehru and others.

Lopez Mateos Wins Presidency

Adolfo Lopez Mateos was elected president July 6, 1959 in the heaviest and most peaceful voting in Mexican history. It was the first presidential election in which women voted. Lopez Mateos received 2,046,568 votes, to 245,083 for his chief opponent, Luis H. Alvarez, 38, of the rightist PAN *(Partido de Accion Nacional,* or National Action Party). An estimated 9 million votes were cast. A new congress of 60 senators and 162 deputies was also elected, with the PRI winning, as usual, both the Senate and the Chamber of Deputies.

Lopez Mateos was inaugurated as Mexico's 57th president in Mexico City Dec. 1. The ceremony was attended by U.S. State Secy. John Foster Dulles in the midst of heavy precautions against threatened left-wing demonstrations. Police had seized a hand press and 100,000 leaflets containing anti-U.S. propaganda and had arrested Miguel Aroche Para, a Mexican Workers Party (Communist front) leader, as well as 6 other Communists in Mexico City Nov. 28.

Lopez Mateos named the following to his new cabinet: *Foreign Minister*—Manuel Tello; *Finance*—Antonio Ortiz Mena; *Communications*—Javier Barros Sierra; *Interior*—Gustavo Diaz Ordaz; *Education*—Jaime Torres Bodet; *Labor*—Salmon Gonzalez Blanco; *Health*—Dr. Alvarez Amezquita; *Economy*—Raul Salinas Lozano; *Social Security*—Benito

Coquet; *Agriculture*—Julian Rodriguez Adame; *Hydraulic Resources*—Alfredo de Mazo; *Defense*—Gen. Agustin Olachea; *Attorney General*—Fernando Lopez Arias; *Navy*—Adm. Manuel Zermeno Araico; *Secretary of the Presidency*—Donato Miranda Fonesca; *National Properties*—Eduardo Bustamente; *Agrarian Affairs*—Prof. Roberto Barrios. Pascual Gutierrez Roldan was appointed to head Pemex *(Petroleos Mexicanos)*, the state oil industry.

(Another round of elections, the triennial congressional elections, took place in 1961. $6\frac{1}{2}$ million Mexican voters cast ballots July 2, 1961 in elections for the 178-seat Chamber of Deputies and for 5 state governorships. The PRI won all 178 seats and all 5 governorships. The elections were untroubled.)

EXPANDED INTERNATIONAL ROLE

One of Lopez Mateo's major goals was to broaden Mexico's contacts with foreign countries. Although Mexico had strengthened its "Good Neighbor" relationship with the U.S. since the Aleman-Truman talks of 1947, many Mexicans, especially in government and industry, desired to see more ties between Mexico and major powers besides the U.S. The motives behind Lopez Mateos, diplomatic offensive were largely economic: Mexico was involved in a major industrial push forward and needed more economic aid. Lopez Mateos also sought to sponsor Mexico as a leader within the new Latin American common market, LAFTA (Lation-American Free Trade Association), formed in 1961. Moreover, it was called imperative that Mexico, as one of the new economic community's most powerful members, reassure its friends in the European Common Market (EEC) that LAFTA did not intend to inaugurate an area of narrow economic protectionism in Latin America.

Visits with U.S. Presidents

Lopez Mateos' first diplomatic move was to meet with U.S. Pres. Dwight D. Eisenhower.

Eisenhower visited Lopez Mateos in Acapulco Feb. 19-20, 1959. The 2 presidents conferred informally during an afternoon cruise on Lopez Mateos' yacht Feb. 19, met with ex-British Prime Min. Anthony Eden at a dinner given by Lopez Mateos at the Mirador Hotel the same evening and conferred Feb. 20 at the Pierre Marques Hotel, where Eisenhower was lodged. Eisenhower left Acapulco by plane just before midnight Feb. 20.

The 2 presidents said in a joint statement Feb. 20 that they had agreed: (1) "that their governments should cooperate and consult together" in efforts to protect both countries' interests in cotton, "Mexico's major export commodity and one of great importance" to the U.S.; (2) "that both countries should contine to study ways to reach a multilateral solution" to the lead and zinc problem; (3) "to plan a coordinated attack on the screwworm problem" and "to explore the feasibility of a joint program of eradication, utilizing radioactive isotopes." The joint statement also disclosed that they had agreed to cooperate in building the $100 million Diablo Dam on the Rio Grande near Del Rio, Tex. The dam was to be 250 feet high and $6\frac{1}{2}$ miles long and was to supplement the Falcon Dam, nearly 100 miles southeast of the new project.

Lopez Mateos, accompanied by his wife and daughter, Eva, 17, paid visits to the U.S. Oct. 9-15 and 18 and to Canada Oct. 15-18. He visited Eisenhower Oct. 9-12, spending part of Oct. 10-11 at the latter's Camp David retreat in Maryland. (It was disclosed Oct. 12 that Eisenhower had given Lopez Mateos a $2,300 blue Ford Falcon sedan, which he [Eisenhower] had paid for himself.) Addressing a special meeting of the OAS Oct. 12, Lopez Mateos said the organization's economic efforts had "not satisfied the legitimate aspirations of our peoples nor the confidence they have placed in our organization." Lopez Mateos visited Chicago Oct. 13, addressed a meeting of the UN General Assembly in New York Oct. 14 and then went to Canada, becoming the first Mexican head of state to do so. He returned to the U.S. Oct. 18 for a barbecue party with ex-Pres. Harry S.

Truman on the Johnson City, Tex. branch of U.S. Senate Democratic leader Lyndon B. Johnson. (Lopez Mateos already knew Johnson. The 2 had met while Lopez Mateos was Ruiz Cortines' labor minister.)

Lopez Mateos met once again briefly with Eisenhower. Eisenhower flew Oct. 24, 1960 to Del Rio, Tex., where midway on the international bridge connecting Del Rio with the Mexican town of Ciudad Acuna, he was greeted by Lopez Mateos. The 2 presidents then announced in Ciudad Acuna that they had agreed to build a new dam, to be known as the Amistad Dam, about 10 miles upstream on the Rio Grande. The Amistad ("friendship") Dam was to supplement the Diablo Dam in controlling and harnessing the Rio Grande.

After John F. Kennedy succeeded Eisenhower as President of the U.S., the Lopez Mateos and the Kennedy administrations solved 2 outstanding but essentially minor disputes between Mexico and the U.S. The resulting accords, barely noticed in the larger nation, were hailed as diplomatic triumphs by patriotic Mexicans. The 2 disputes—over the salinity of the Colorado River and over title to the Chamizal border area—were settled by Lopez Mateos and Kennedy during a state visit made by Kennedy to Lopez Mateos in Mexico City June 29-July 1, 1962. (A U.S. loan of $20 million for Mexican agriculture was also announced.)

A joint communique issued June 30 gave these details of the discussions:

Affirmation of democracy—"Both presidents reaffirmed the dedication of their countries to the ideals of individual liberty and personal dignity which constitute the foundation of a civilization which they share in common. In consonance with their dedication to these ideals, and acting always as sovereign and independent countries, . . . they propose to respect and maintain the principles of non-intervention—whether this intervention may come from a continental or extra-continental state—and of self-determination of peoples.

"Therefore they are resolved to uphold these principles in the international organizations to which they belong, to defend and strengthen the democratic institutions which their peoples have constructed, and to oppose totalitarian institutions and activities which are incompatible with the democratic principles they uphold."

Hemispheric system supported—"Both presidents fully accept the responsibility of every sovereign nation to form its own policies, without outside dictation or coercion. They also recognize that the republics of the hemisphere share the commitment they have freely accepted, in accordance with the Inter-American Treaty of Reciprocal Assistance and the Charter of the Organization of American States, to defend the continent and to foster fundamental democratic values. This principle of common responsibility, without impairment of national independence, is the cornerstone of the Organization of American States.

"Another dimension of this principle was expressed at the Punta del Este conference in Aug. 1961. The 2 presidents reaffirm their support of the Charter of Punta del Este and of the program of accelerated social and economic progress which that charter embodies. Mexico and the United States, together with the other countries of the inter-American system, are closely associated in a vast endeavor, without precedent, to promote the well-being of all the inhabitants of the hemisphere."

Alliance for Progress—"Pres. Kennedy recognized that the fundamental goal of the Mexican Revolution is the same as that of the Alliance for Progress—social justice and economic progress within the framework of individual freedom and political liberty.

"The 2 presidents discussed the economic and social development program of Mexico. Pres. Kennedy reaffirmed his country's commitment, made in the Charter of Punta del Este, to continue to cooperate with the government of Mexico in the endeavor which it and the Mexico people are carrying out to accelerate the economic and social well-being of all the inhabitants of the Republic. . . . Mexico and the United States are determined . . . to continue the effort until hunger, poverty, illiteracy and social injustice have been eliminated from this hemisphere."

Commodity exports—"The 2 heads of state concurred in the need for intensifying the efforts which are being made through the various international organizations, including the United Nations, the inter-American system and the European Economic Community, to achieve expanding levels of trade, with special attention to the elimination of discriminatory and restrictive practices against exports of basic commodities from Latin America.

"They agreed that it is indispensable that a broadened and more stable market should be provided in order to improve the income of the exporting countries. Of such income, workers and farmers should have an equitable share to permit increases in their levels of living. . . ."

The UN & disarmament—"The 2 heads of state exchanged views on the importance of the UN in promoting international understanding and peace and in encouraging economic and social progress. They decided that their governments should consult each other with a view to cooperating even more closely in all matters which maintain and strengthen the purposes and principles of the San Francisco Charter.

"Both Presidents expressed the strong desire that, within the scope of the UN and particularly at Geneva, negotiations should continue for general disarmament as well as for the termination of nuclear tests, both based upon effective means of control. . . ."

Chamizal dispute. "The 2 presidents discussed the problem of Chamizal. They agreed to instruct their executive agencies to recommend a complete solution to this problem which, without prejudice to their juridical position, takes into account the entire history of this tract."

Colorado River salinity—"In relation to the problem of salinity of the

waters of the Colorado River, the 2 presidents discussed the studies which
have been conducted by scientists of the 2 countries. The 2 presidents noted
that water which the U.S.A. plans to release during the winter of 1962-63
for river regulation, and such other measures as may be immediately feasible,
should have the beneficial effect of reducing the salinity of the waters until
Oct. 1963. They expressed their determination . . . to reach a permanent and
effective solution at the earliest possible time with the aim of preventing the
recurrence of this problem after Oct. 1963. . . .''

Kennedy issued a separate statement announcing the
agriculture loan: "Improvement of the life of the *campesino*
[farmer] is one of the central goals of the Mexican Revolution, and a major part of the Alliance for Progress. Mexico
has carried forward the largest and most impressive land reform program in the entire history of the hemisphere. Since
the beginning of your revolution more than 133 million acres
of land have been distributed to almost 2 million people. And
never has this program been more vigorously administered
than during the last 3 years, when the government of Lopez
Mateos distributed 24 million acres to hundreds of thousands
of *campesinos*. The tangible results of your land reform can
be witnessed in the 223% rise in agricultural output over the
last 2 decades—a rise which has made Mexico virtually self-
sufficient in foodstuffs. . . . This $20 million loan . . . is an-
other reaffirmation of my country's unyielding and continuing commitment to work with the Mexican government in
its vast development effort to provide more jobs for its
workers, a better life for its farmers, and to help Mexico rise
to its inevitable high rank among the industrialized nations
of the world. . . .''

The Colorado River dispute developed after a 1944 treaty
under which Mexico was allowed to take $1\frac{1}{2}$ million acre-
feet of water from the river annually for irrigation. Arizona's
Welton-Mohawk drainage and irrigation project, however,
had caused a flow of saline water from the Gila River into
the Colorado. Mexican agronomists had reported in Feb. 1961
that, as a result, 25,000 acres in the Mexicali valley had been
contaminated by salinity. The Lopez Mateos-Kennedy talks
led to an agreement whereby the U.S. would recognize an
obligation to reduce Colorado River salinity by the addition
of fresh water "flushes."

The Chamizal dispute involved a border area of 630 acres on the Rio Grande river between El Paso, Tex. and Ciudad Juarez in Mexico. As a result of erosion, it had become unclear which nation possessed sovereignty over which sections of the Chamizal. By 1961 the Chamizal already had a population of 8,000. Washington and Mexico City announced July 18, 1963 the formal settlement of the long-standing dispute. Chamizal zone under the provisions of a joint memorandum: (1) 437 acres of the disputed area would pass from U.S. to Mexican sovereignty; (2) the U.S. would retain 133 acres; (3) about 3,500 displaced U.S. citizens would be resettled in El Paso; (4) the U.S. would pay $28 million for transferred real estate; (5) the U.S. would spend $18 million and Mexico $10 million to alter the course of the Rio Grande. The agreement was ratified by the Mexican and U.S. Senates and became effective Dec. 17, 1963.

The settlement of the Chamizal dispute was received with national celebrations in Mexico. It was regarded by many as adding considerably to Lopez Mateos' prestige.

Lopez Mateos conferred with Kennedy's sucessor, U.S. Pres. Lyndon B. Johnson, in California Feb. 21-22, 1964. The 2 heads of state then disclosed in a joint communique that Colorado River salinity (still spoiling Mexican land) and increased hemisphere trade had been the main topics of the talks.

Both men spoke at the 96th Charter Day anniversary celebration of the University of California at Los Angeles Feb. 21 and attended a fiesta Feb. 22 at the Los Angeles Sports Arena arranged by Lopez Mateos on the theme of Mexican-U.S. friendship. In his UCLA address Johnson said that the "revolutions" in the U.S. and Mexico would not end "so long as there remains a man without a job, a family without a roof, a child without a school, . . . while any American is denied his rights because of the color of his skin, . . . while any American is jobless, hungry, uneducated and ignored." Lopez Mateos, speaking at the UCLA convocation in Spanish, said that "the most pressing problem of our time consists in finding equilibrium for the prodigious amount of

technical and scientific data—now dispersed around the world
—with a juridical order in which we can conciliate the freedom of the human person and the open and firm decision to
remove social injustice." Both presidents received honorary
law doctorates at the ceremony. They then flew to Palm
Springs for private consultations and paid a social call on the
ex-Pres. Eisenhower at nearby Palm Desert.

At a news conference in Palm Springs Feb. 22 Lopez
Mateos offered Mexico's "best efforts" to mediate the dispute
between the U.S. and Panama over the Panama Canal. He
held that the dispute could be handled best within the Organization of American States (OAS). On the U.S.-Cuba dispute, however, he suggested that "since Cuba has been ousted
from the OAS," the U.S. should turn to the UN "to find a
solution of its problems with Cuba."

At the Mexican fiesta in Los Angeles Feb. 22, Johnson
spoke of the nearness in purpose of his domestic "war on
poverty" and the Alliance for Progress programs and Lopez
Mateos' programs in Mexico. Lopez Mateos flew back to
Mexico City after the fiesta.

Hemispheric Cooperation

Mexico played one of the major roles in negotiations to
ease trade among the countries of Latin America. The resulting agreement, to create a 7-nation free trade zone, was
signed in Montevideo, Uruguay Feb. 18, 1960, and it went
into effect May 2 as delegates from Argentina, Brazil, Chile,
Mexico, Paraguay, Peru and Uruguay deposited instruments
of ratification in Montevideo.

The accord, known as the Treaty of Montevideo, provided for the formation of a Latin-American Free Trade Association (LAFTA) somewhat similar to the European Economic Community (EEC) established by the Treaty of Rome.
(LAFTA is known in Spanish by the acronym ALALC, for
Asociacion Latino-Americana de Libre Comercio.) The free trade
provisions were not as extensive as those of the EEC, however.
Mexico, along with Brazil and Argentina, indicated its expec-

tations of becoming a leader in the new group. The objectives of LAFTA, as stated in the preamble of the treaty, include "the expansion of present national markets, through the gradual elimination of barriers to intra-regional trade," perseverance in "efforts to establish, gradually and progressively, a Latin American Common Market," and the pooling of "efforts to achieve the progressive complementarity and integration of their national economies on the basis of an effective reciprocity of benefits."

The treaty, which exempted agriculture and livestock trade, would (1) eliminate over a 12-year period restrictions on at least 75% of trade among member countries; (2) require each pact member to submit a list of goods on which it would reduce tariffs by at least 8% immediately and to make a similar reduction each subsequent year (although the type of goods could be changed each year); (3) require the establishment every 3 years of a common list of irremovable goods representing 25% of the area's trade. A provisional free-trade association was established in Montevideo, which became the permanent home of the trade group.

LAFTA proved to be Mexico's 4th largest market for export earnings in 1961, but Mexican products yielded approximately 20 times more in the U.S. than they earned in all the LAFTA nations combined. (Mexico accounted for only 1% of the interzonal commerce among the LAFTA nations during the period 1952-61, but by 1966 the Mexican share of such trade had risen to 6.3%. These nations had joined LAFTA by 1972: Argentina, Bolivia, Brazil, Chile, Colombia, Equador, Mexico, Paraguay, Peru, Uruguay and Venezuela.)

Mexico, along with most other Latin American nations, joined the U.S.-initiated Alliance for Progress *(Allianza para el Progreso)* in Aug. 1961. The Alliance for Progress, a plan to combat the spread of communism in Latin America, had been announced by U.S. Pres. John F. Kennedy in his 1961 inauguration address. The plan offered economic and technical aid to "our sister republics south of the border." The Alliance for Progress, conceived as an antidote to Cuban Castroism, was approved overwhelmingly by the countries

of Latin America at an Inter-American Economic & Social
Conference in Punta del Este. Uruguay in Aug. 1961. The
Alliance Charter, implementing the plan, and an accompanying Declaration of Punta del Este, summarizing the charter's
goals, were adopted by the conference Aug. 16. The documents were signed by representatives of Mexico, the U.S.
and 18 other American countries at the conclusion of the
conference Aug. 17 (Cuba refused to sign the documents.)

Figures published in Mar. 1962 showed that funds committed by the U.S. to Mexico under the Alliance for Progress
between Mar. 1961 and Feb. 1962 amounted to $106,321,000.
Of this total, $95,780,000 was provided by the U.S. Export-
Import Bank. (Only Brazil received more.)

Mexican-Guatemalan Shrimp-Boat Dispute

Lopez Mateos announced Jan. 23, 1959 that Mexico had
broken diplomatic relations with Guatemala because of the
Dec. 31, 1958 strafing of Mexican shrimp boats by the Guatemalan air force in the Pacific off Champerico, Guatemala.
3 Mexican fishermen had been killed, 14 wounded and 11 arrested in the incident. Guatemala had rejected several Mexican
protests on grounds that the ships were within its territorial
waters, which the Guatemalan Government claimed extended
12 miles from shore. In a nationwide address Jan. 25, Guatemalan Pres. Miguel Ydigoras Fuentes charged Mexico with
massing "air, sea and land military forces on our maritime and
land borders." He defended the strafing, saying that "our maritime riches in our territorial waters have been robbed continu-
ously and pitilessly for years." The Mexican Defense Ministry
denied to the UN Jan. 27 that any troop concentrations had
taken place. An international bridge linking Guatemala and
Mexico was destroyed by Guatemalans Jan. 29 in an anti-
Mexican demonstration. It was also charged by Guatemalan-
Amb-to-Mexico Col. Arturo Ramirez Pinto Jan. 9 that a
ccnspiracy to overthrow the Guatemalan government was
based in Mexico.

Diplomatic relations with Guatemala were resumed

Sept. 15 after an 8-month hiatus.

Lopez Mateos in Europe

Lopez Mateos made a European tour, including a number of state visits, Mar. 26-Apr. 8, 1963.

The Mexican president began Mar. 26-29 with a visit to France, where he conferred with French Pres. Charles de Gaulle. A joint communique, issued Mar. 28 after the talks between Lopez Mateos and Charles de Gaulle said:

It was agreed that the time had come to strengthen cooperation not only between France and Mexico, but also between all the nations of Latin origin and tradition, which are united by a common culture and by the same principles of freedom. . . .

The problem of developing countries was discussed with particular attention. It is the great problem of our times. It is the duty of the highly industrialized countries to cooperate with those which are less so. . . .

Gen. de Gaulle and Pres. Lopez Mateos noted with satisfaction the successful outcome of the Franco-Mexican negotiations concerning French participation in the economic development of Mexico, and more particularly of its petrochemical industry. They agreed on the creation of a joint Franco-Mexican commission which will . . . be responsible for deciding on the development projects which France will help to finance. . . .

The 2 heads of state examined the conditions in which fruitful cooperation could develop between the 2 regional systems . . . of which France and Mexico are members—the European Economic Community and the Latin American Free Trade Area [LAFTA]. They agreed that the aims of the Treaty of Rome and the Treaty of Montevideo were comparable—*viz.*, to assure social and economic progress, improve the conditions of life and work, and contribute to the progressive abolition of restrictions on international exchanges. Thus the common interest of France and Mexico demands that these 2 international organizations should work in a spirit of positive cooperation.

Lopez Mateos arrived in Belgrade, the Yugoslav capital, Mar. 29 for talks with Pres. Tito. It was the first time a Latin American head of state had payed a state visit to the neutralist Communist nation. A joint communique issued Apr. 1 stressed Yugoslav-Mexican agreement on peace and disarmament. Tito accepted an invitation to visit Mexico (and he did so in Oct. 1963).

Lopez then visited Poland Apr. 1-2 and conferred with Premier Joszef Cyrankiewicz. (Cyrankiewicz had visited Mexico briefly a month earlier). A joint communique issued in Warsaw Apr. 2 noted the common opposition of the 2 republics to protectionist policies in world trade.

Lopez Apr. 3-4 visited Holland, where he was received by Queen Juliana and where he arranged with government leaders for a loan of $60 million dollars for the construction of a new Pacific port at Mazatlan.

The Mexican president's final European visit of the trip was to the German Federal Republic (West Germany) Apr. 5-7. He talked with Vice Chancellor Ludwig Erhard, touching mainly upon EEC-LAFTA economic cooperation. A joint communique issued Apr. 7 said that the West German government would try to facilitate German credit extension and capital investment in Mexico.

Lopez Mateos returned to Mexico Apr. 8.

De Gaulle's Visit

French Pres. Charles de Gaulle paid a 4-day visit to Mexico Mar. 16-19, 1964 before visiting the French possessions of Guadaloupe, Martinique and French Guiana. De Gaulle was said to have gone to Mexico because of his desire for more international prestige for France rather because of a specific Mexican request. (De Gaulle had been planning a South American tour as well since 1963.)

Mexico actually traded very little with France, considerably less in 1964 than with Switzerland and West Germany. But one aim of the Franco-Mexican talks—aside from considerations of diplomatic prestige for both sides—was to foster greater mutual understanding between the French government which considered itself the paramount force in the European Common Market (EEC), and the Mexican government, which saw itself performing a similar role in the Latin American economic community (LAFTA).

Landing in Merida, Mexico Mar. 16, de Gaulle changed from the U.S. Presidential Boeing 707 airliner to a French-built Caravelle jet for the flight to Mexico City. He was greeted by Lopez Mateos and hailed by enthusiastic crowds of Mexicans on his arrival at the capital's International Airport and during his drive into the city in an open car. Addressing an estimated 225,000 persons from a balcony of the National Palace, de Gaulle, speaking in Spanish, called emotionally for a new era of French-Mexican cooperation. The 2 nations shared common ideals and "feel themselves destined-to the same future," he said. "Let us walk hand in hand."

De Gaulle and Lopez Mateos began 3 days of intermittent private talks later Mar. 16. De Gaulle's public itinerary Mar. 17 included an address to the Permanent Commission of the Mexican Congress (the interim legislative body during Congressional recesses) and visits to the Mexican Independence Monument and to a government housing project. In his speech to the Commission, he emphasized France's determination to build new ties with Mexico but without affecting Mexico's traditional relationship with the U.S.

A joint communique issued by the 2 leaders Mar. 18 pledged new efforts to strengthen not only Mexico's ties with France but the ties between the wider Latin and European communities, particularly between members of LAFTA and the EEC. The communique said that France and Mexico would study measures to increase their trade and cultural exchanges and would create an interparliamentary commission to deal with French-Mexican problems. It indicated that the 2 leaders had examined the possibility of a greater volume of French investment in Mexico in cooperation with Mexican capital. The communique said:

> . . . The 2 presidents resumed the examination, begun in Paris a year ago, of the problem of developing countries. They recognized the importance in this respect of the UN Conference on Trade & Development . . ., one of the objects of which is to seek trade policies capable of modifying the conditions in which trade exchanges take place between countries with a high standard of living and those in process of industrialization.

> Gen. de Gaulle stated that France was preparing to present to the conference original formulas both for primary products and manufactured or semi-manufactured products from developing countries, in particular those of Latin America. Pres. Lopez Mateos . . . emphasized the necessity for the more developed countries to examine with great attention the points of view which the developing countries, especially the group of Latin American countries, will put forward at Geneva to ensure a healthy expansion of the world economy. The 2 heads of state agreed that Mexico and France should unite their efforts to contribute to the solution of this problem.

> Franco-Mexican relations were examined in the spirit of cooperation which inspires the 2 governments. . . . A common determination was expressed

to neglect nothing which could reinforce mutual exchanges in all spheres. It was especially noted with satisfaction that the plan to establish inter-parliamentary meetings has been realized by the creation of a Franco-Mexican Committee for Parliamentary Affairs.

Gen. de Gaulle and Pres. Lopez Mateos considered that Franco-Mexican cooperation, already well begun on the economic plane, should be intensified in the cultural sphere. . . . The size of the effort accomplished in this direction is already considerable. . . . They noted with satisfaction that the number of scholarships awarded to Mexicans by the French government is increasingly large and that the Mexican government intends to increase to a considerable extent the number of scholarships which it awards to French students.

The 2 governments noted with satisfaction that technical cooperation has assumed much importance, as shown by the help given by French experts in training centers in Mexico and by the number of Mexicans pursuing higher training studies in France. They considered that important possibilities for developing [this cooperation] exist in such fields as planning, agriculture, and electronics. . . .

In the light of the conclusions of the Cooperation Commission created at their meeting in Paris, which met in Mexico from Feb. 17-28, the 2 heads of state examined Franco-Mexican economic relations. They expressed satisfaction at the increase, particularly marked in 1963, of the volume of exchanges, and agreed that the agreement prepared by this commission . . . should be signed in the near future. . . .

In expressing his interest in the efforts being made by the Latin American countries for their development, Gen. de Gaulle indicated that France recognized the role which she could play in the development of the continent thanks to the ancient links which bind her to these countries.

The evolution of the Common Market and the part which it is equally called upon to play in this historic work were studied in the same spirit. It is clear that a powerful and expanding economy like that of the EEC will favor the development of exchanges with Latin American. It was recognized as desirable that the EEC and LAFTA should follow the path of cooperation for their mutual benefit.

. . . The 2 heads of state considered that the contacts established should be maintained in future. For this purpose, regular consultations between the 2 governments will be organized in all spheres, notably in those of foreign policy, economic affairs, trade, and culture. . . .

De Gaulle visited the National Autonomous University of Mexico and addressed the National Chamber of Commerce in Mexico City Mar. 18. De Gaulle's Mexico visit ended Mar. 19 with a trip to Aztec ruins near the capital and with an airport farewell attended by Lopez Mateos, Mexican cabinet members and foreign diplomats.

Visits From Other Statesmen

Prime Min. Jawaharlal Nehru of India paid a state visit

to Mexico Nov. 15-17, 1961. Nehru addressed a joint session of the Mexican congress; he praised the Mexican Revolution and said that India had drawn inspiration from it in its own struggle for independence.

Pres. Joao Goulart of Brazil, accompained by Foreign Min. Francisco San Tiago Dantas and Finance Min. Walter Moreira Salles, paid a state visit to Mexico Apr. 8-9, 1962 following a visit to the U.S. Goulart, the first Brazilian head of state to visit Mexico officially, was hailed by large crowds on his way from the airport into Mexico City Apr. 8. But he left Mexico the next day because of sudden ill health.

Yugoslav Pres. Tito, 71, visited Mexico, Brazil, Bolivia and Chile Sept. 18-Oct. 16, 1964. The purpose of Tito's Mexican visit was to appeal for closer trade relations and to seek support for his policy of non-alignment. His accompanying party included his wife, Foreign Min. Koca Popovic and Parliament Vice Pres. Mijalko Todorovic. Tito arrived in Merida, Mexico Oct. 3 and then flew Oct. 4 to Mexico City, where he was greeted by Lopez Mateos. After trips to Guadalajara and Acapulco, Tito flew to Washington Oct. 16. Lopez Mateos and Tito had called on the UN to "deliberate what measures should be taken to reach a general agreement on non-intervention and relations and cooperation between states." They stressed "the need to guarantee to less-developed countries the right to get just prices for their products and to have greater access to international financial resources and the latest achievements of science and technology."

CUBA, THE U.S. & MEXICO

It was from Yucatan State in Mexico that Fidel Castro's July 26 Movement had sailed to Cuba in its unsuccessful 1953 revolt. When Castro seized power from Cuban dictator Juan Batista Jan. 1, 1959, many Mexicans simply assumed that the new Cuban revolution would be a recapitulation, with a dash of Caribbean flavor, of their own revered Mexican Revolution. Mexico recognized the Castro government and retained high-level diplomatic contact even during the period of the

deepest Soviet penetration of the island republic. Although
Fidel Castro's popularity in Mexico waned as his dependency
on the Soviets grew, many Mexicans continued to support
the essential ideas of the Cuban Revolution, holding that its
pro-Soviet leaning was merely a passing phase.

Mexican radicals have continued to support the Cuban
Revolution and some have participated in the personality cult
of *Fidelismo*. With a powerful radical wing within the PRI,
even the PRI's anti-Castro elements have softened their con-
demnations of Castro in the interests of party unity. But most
members of the PRI, whether conservative or radical, are
said to agree on this oft-quoted formula: "Mexico does not
export or import revolution."

Mexican Position Unclear

The spectre of the Cuban problem began to trouble U.S.-
Mexican relations in 1960 when U.S.-Cuban antagonisms
flared over Cuba's seizure of U.S. property, over Castro's
mounting collaboration with the Soviet bloc and over mutual
U.S.-Cuban charges of aggressive intent.

Mexican Chamber of Deputies Pres. Emilio Sanchez
Piedras and Senate leader Manuel Moreno Sanchez stated
publicly in early July several times that Mexico would back
Cuba against the U.S. The statements were made without any
apparent government authorization. Foreign Min. Manuel
Tello, a close associate of Lopez Mateos, said in Mexico City
July 11 that these statements definitely did not express govern-
ment policy on the Cuban question.

Meanwhile, in Washington, the Mexican representative
to the OAS (Organization of American States) joined the 20
other representatives July 18 in approving a unanimous resolution to hold a foreign ministers' meeting to consider
"threats" to continental solidarity, regional defense and democratic principles. At the resulting Latin American foreign
ministers' conference in San Jose, Costa Rica Aug. 28, all 19
represented countries voted to approve a resolution supporting the U.S. stand against Cuba. (Mexico, however, noted

reservations.)

The document known as the "Declaration of San Jose," did not mention Cuba. It was thoroughly understood, however, that the declaration was indeed intended as criticism of Castro for accepting Soviet military protection against the U.S. The Mexican delegation, however, chose to interpret the declaration in a highly ambiguous way. It was widely believed that the Mexicans wished to uphold the principle of non-intervention without challenging the U.S. too harshly.

Before leaving San Jose Aug. 29, U.S. State Secy. Christian Herter said the declaration was a clear indictment of . . . Cuba and particularly the role which it has played in furthering the Sino-Soviet efforts of intervention into this hemisphere." The Mexican delegation frankly disagreed, claiming that the declaration was of "a general character and not "a condemnation or a threat against Cuba. . . ."

The conference Aug. 28 had also voted to establish a 6-nation committee to investigate Caribbean disputes, "especially" U.S.-Cuban controversies, and to offer its good offices in settling them. The committee's members: Mexico, Costa Rica, Colombia, Venezuela, Brazil and Chile.

Mexico's stand in the dispute was further clouded by incidents that occurred during independence festivities in Sept. 1960. 3 U.S. Congress members attending Mexico's 150th independence anniversary celebration temporarily boycotted official functions Sept. 14 in protest against a pro-Cuban speech made the same day in congress by Emilio Sanchez Piedras, president of the Mexican Chamber of Deputies. In his speech welcoming foreign delegates to the celebration, Sanchez lauded the Cuban revolution for freeing Cuba "from outside forces as sinister as Nazism, fascism and Francoism." Sens. Kenneth B. Keating (R., N.Y.) and Thomas Dodd (D., Conn.) and Rep. John R. Rhodes (R., Ariz.) protested that Sanchez had "left a clear impression that this outside influence, in the case of Cuba, was the United States." They said, however, that they had been assured of Mexico's friendship for the U.S. after attending a reception given Sept. 16 in their honor by Mexican Senate leader Manuel Moreno

Sanchez.

Relations between Cuba and the U.S. deteriorated during 1960. In 1961 the U.S. ended direct diplomatic contacts with Cuba. Among factors that led to the break, in addition to Castro's growing ties to the Soviet bloc were: U.S. fears of Castro-fomented uprisings throughout Latin America; Castro's "vilification" of the U.S.; Castro's seizure of U.S. assets in Cuba; Castro's attacks on U.S. rights to the Guantanamo naval base; the U.S.' refusal to renew its Cuban sugar-purchase contracts: Cuban fears of a U.S.-based invasion.

The *N.Y. Times* reported Jan. 22, 1961 that Mexican troops and navy ships had started to patrol the Yucatan Peninsula to thwart any possible use of Mexican territory or territorial waters for military moves by Cubans for or against the Castro regime.

An anti-Castro force landed on the swampy beaches of Cuba's southern Las Villas Province before dawn Apr. 17 in an attack directed by the U.S.-based National Revolutionary Council. The rebels, supported by planes, made their principal landing in the area of Bahia de Cochinos (Bay of Pigs) in southern Las Villas Province, but the expedition proved to be a fiasco, and the invaders were quickly overcome by Castro's forces.

At the UN, Mexican delegate Luis Padilla Nervo Apr. 18 introduced a resolution appealing to all countries "to ensure that their territories and resources are not used to promote the civil war in Cuba."

The landings touched off anti-U.S. riots and pro-Castro demonstrations throughout Mexico, Latin America and Europe Apr. 17-22. The largest Latin-American demonstrations occurred Apr. 21 in Mexico City. About 1,000 soldiers, police and firemen intercepted 15,000 Castro sympathizers who were marching on the National Palace. 150 demonstrators were injured, and 200 were arrested.

Mexico Backs U.S. in Missile Crisis

One of the most perilous Soviet-U.S. confrontations of

the cold war took place late in 1962 in the Caribbean. The
U.S., announcing that it had discovered offensive Soviet
missile bases under construction in Cuba, blockaded the island and demanded the removal of the bases. For 6 days the
world lived in fear of an armed clash between the 2 great
powers. Then the Soviet government announced that it would
dismantle the launching sites and withdraw its missiles. By
the year's end, U.S. reconnaissance planes had verified
Russia's removal of 42 medium-range missiles and 42 jet
bombers.

The Mexican government tried to maintain a neutral
position in the U.S.-Cuban quarrel. Yet however sympathetic Mexican leaders were to both Cuba and the U.S., they
indicated that they were decidedly opposed to Soviet penetration into the hemisphere. Thus, as far as the U.S.-*Soviet* dispute was concerned, the Mexican government sided with the
U.S. During the "Cuban missile crisis" Mexico never specifically condemned the Cuban revolutionary regime but only the
presence of Russian arms in Cuba. (Mexico, as a signatory of
the 1947 Inter-American Treaty of Reciprocal Assistance, was
under an international obligation to come to the assistance
of any other signatory power menaced by any nonhemisphere
power.)

An OAS council on the ministerial level was convened
Oct. 23 and issued a resolution demanding an end to Soviet
penetration in Cuba. The resolution: (1) Urged the immediate dismantling and withdrawal from Cuba of all missiles
and other weapons with any offensive capability"; (2) re-
commended that the OAS "take all measures individually
and collectively, including the use of armed force, to ensure
that . . . Cuba cannot continue to receive from the Sino-
Soviet powers material . . . which may threaten the peace and
security of the continent and to prevent the missiles in Cuba
with offensive capability from ever becoming an active threat
to the [continent's] peace and security"; (3) announced the
OAS Council's decision "to inform" the UN Security Council
of this resolution in "the hope that the Security Council will
. . . dispatch UN observers to Cuba at the earliest moment";

(4) announced the OAS Council's plan "to continue to act provisionally as the Organ of Consultation and to urge member states to keep the Organ of Consultation duly informed of the measures adopted in accordance with Paragraph 2 of this resolution."

The resolution was approved unanimously. In voting for the resolution, Mexico subscribed to an armed American blockade (described as a "quarantine") of Russian-escorted munitions ships to Cuba. The Mexican vote did not approve any specific censure of the Cuban revolutionary government or Cuba's right to defend itself against foreign intervention. On the same day, Oct. 23, a letter was sent by Lopez Mateos to Cuban Pres. Osvaldo Dorticos Torrado with the aim of clarifying the Mexican government's position. The letter explained that Mexico could not view with indifference a Latin-American country establishing facilities for the utilization of the most destructive weapons of all times."

Abstention on Anti-Cuban Resolutions

Mexico has abstained in most anti-Cuba resolutions adopted by organizations of Latin American or Western Hemisphere states. Among developments surrounding these abstentions :

The foreign ministers of the Organization of American States voted Jan. 30-31, 1962 to exclude Cuba "from participation in the inter-American system." They did so on the grounds that Cuba's self-proclaimed adherence to Marxism-Leninism was "incompatible with the principles and objectives of the inter-American system" and that Cuba's "alignment ... with the Communist bloc breaks the unity and solidarity of the hemisphere." The ministers' action, designed to exclude Cuba from OAS activities but not to deprive Cuba of OAS membership, was taken at the final sessions of an OAS foreign ministers' conference begun Jan. 22 in Punta del Este, Uruguay. The U.S. had fought for stronger action against Cuba and had accepted compromises only in the hope of having the resolution adopted with near unanimity. The resolution excluding Cuba from OAS participation was approved by 14-1 vote with Mexico and 4 other countries abstaining. Voting for: U.S., Colombia, Venezuela, Peru, Paraguay. Uruguay, Haiti, Dominican Republic, Panama, Honduras, Costa Rica, Nicaragua, Guatemala and El Salvador. Voting against: Cuba. Abstaining (in addition to Mexico): Argentina, Brazil, Chile and Ecuador.

The Council of the OAS July 3, 1963 approved by 14-1 vote a series of recommendations for action to combat alleged Cuban subversion in the Western Hemisphere. Chile voted against; Mexico and these 3 other nations abstained: Brazil, Haiti and Venezuela.

The Latin-American Free Trade Association rejected Cuba's application for LAFTA membership Sept. 4, 1963. The vote was 7-0, with 2 abstentions—Mexico and Brazil.

The OAS foreign ministers, meeting in Washington July 21-26, 1964, voted to impose mandatory economic sanctions on Cuba and to bar OAS members from maintaining diplomatic ties with the Castro government. The vote July 26 in favor of the resolution was 15-4, with Mexico, Bolivia, Chile and Uruguay opposed. A majority (13) of the 19 nations voting was required for adoption. Most delegates indicated a belief that a meaningful majority had been obtained and that this gave impact to the resolution. A vote July 25 at a closed session of the conference's 20-nation general committee had produced a similar tally. The session also approved a Brazil-sponsored "declaration of Washington" stressing the democratic nature of the American system and expressing hope that the Cuban people would put a democratic government in power "through their own means" and "in the nearest possible future." 16 nations voted for this resolution; Mexico, Chile and Bolivia abstained. Mexico, Bolivia, Chile and Uruguay were the only nations in Latin America that still maintained diplomatic relations with Cuba. (A provision banning air traffic to Cuba had been dropped from the resolution as a concession to Mexico's air link with Havana.)

Mexican Foreign Min. Jose Gorostiza announced in a communique Aug. 3, 1964 that Mexico would not be bound by the OAS action barring members from maintaining diplomatic relations with Cuba. He asserted that the OAS did not have authority under the Inter-American Reciprocal Assistance Treaty to order a severing of diplomatic relations. Such action in regard to Cuba "prejudices the necessities of communications and the interests of an infinite number of persons for whom the existence of Latin-American missions in Havana are indispensable," he said. Gorostiza, indicating that he was expressing the views of Pres. Lopez Mateos, said that Mexico would accept "without reserve" any decision of the International Court of Justice if other OAS members brought the Cuban question before that court. Gorostiza's communique did not mention the economic sanctions imposed by the OAS, but Mexico's position was that they violated Article 96 of the UN charter, which banned any sanctions action by regional organizations without UN approval.

Mexico granted political asylum in June 1964 to Juana Castro Ruz, 31, the sister of Cuban Premier Fidel Castro. Miss Castro announced in a TV statement in Mexico City June 29 that she had defected from Cuba and had asked for such asylum in Mexico. "I have broken all bonds with Fidel and Raul [Raul Castro, Fidel's brother]," Miss Castro declared at a press conference in Mexico City June 30. "I will never return to Cuba until it has regained freedom." Miss Castro reportedly had flown from Cuba to Mexico City June 20 via a Cuban Airlines plane with the help of her brother Raul and the government's permission. Castro charged during a reception at the Canadian embassy in Havana July 1 that his sister's TV statement had been written at the U.S. embassy in Mexico City. "This incident is personally very bitter and profoundly painful, but I realize that this is the price of being a revolutionary," Castro declared.

(Fidel Castro had indicated at a July 27 press conference that he would choose Mexico to act as intermediary in any future talks with the U.S.)

Trotsky's Assassin Released

"Jacques Mornard," who had assassinated exiled Russian revolutionist Leon Trotsky in Mexico City in 1940, was released from jail and deported secretly to Cuba by the Mexican government May 6, 1960. He was granted provisional liberty May 4, 2½ months before his 20-year sentence was to expire, to avoid demonstrations or attempts on his life. He was put on a Havana-bound plane in Mexico City by Mexican Interior Ministry officials May 6. Mornard, who used a half-dozen aliases, left Mexico under the name Jacques Mornard van Dendreschd and used a Czechoslovak passport issued to him several months previously. He was accompanied by 2 Czechoslovak embassy officials. (Mexican officials disclosed that the secret deportation had been carried out in the interest of the ex-prisoner's safety.)

No facts concerning the unrevealed identity of the assassin were disclosed by the Mexican government. In fact, "Mornard" had maintained total silence on his mission and identity from his capture to his release 20 years later. "Mornard" had entered Mexico City early in 1940 under the alias "Frank Jacson" and bearing a false Canadian passport. Gaining Trotsky's confidence, he was admitted Aug. 20, 1940, to the Soviet exile's heavily defended villa in the Mexico City suburb of Coyoacan. There he attacked Trotsky from the rear with a mountaineer's icepick and wounded him fatally. A letter discovered on "Mornard" claimed that he was a disillusioned Trotskyite. A Mexican fingerprint expert later claimed that "Mornard's" fingerprints matched those of Ramon del Rio Mercador (or Mercader), an alleged Communist agitator arrested in Barcelona in 1935. Mercador's mother, Caridad Mercador, was said to have been a close friend of Lavrenti Beria, the Georgian-born head of the Soviet secret internal security forces (NKVD), who was executed after Stalin's death.

DOMESTIC UNREST & REFORM

During the early years of the Lopez Mateos administration there was a rise in the activity of Mexican left-wing militants. The reemergence of the Mexican left was a result partly of the appeal of the Castro revolutionary regime in Cuba but also of mounting pressures within Mexican society itself. The vogue of Fidelismo inevitably became intermingled with the ongoing drive of the older Mexican revolutionary movement.

2 champions arose to lead the anti-government struggle. One was David Alfaro Siqueiros, 64, a distinguished muralist who succeeded Diego Rivera as the cultural leader of Mexican Marxists. For a time before his imprisonment, Siqueiros was the nominal head of the approximately 70,000-member Mexican Communist Party. The other champion was veteran Mexican revolutionary hero Lazaro Cardenas, president of the republic 1934-40, initiator of the nationalization of Mexico's petroleum resources in 1938 and dogged defender of the nation's downtrodden landless peasants—referred to variously as *campesinos,* agricultural workers, *peones,* peons or, more popularly, *los de abajo,* the underdogs.

When Lopez Mateos was elected president in 1958 many observers saw him as Cardenas' protege. Ex-presidents are particularly powerful in Mexican politics, and Cardenas had been one of Lopez Mateos' sponsors for PRI nomination. Moreover, in 1958, in the traditional pre-election stumping mandatory for PRI presidential candidates despite the lack of a serious opposition, Lopez Mateos had repeatedly called for improvement in the living conditions of Mexico's backward agricultural laborers. This sounded like a clear echo of Cardenas, who himself had spearheaded the populist revival in rural Mexico during the 1930s.

Lopez Mateos did initiate a major agrarian reform in 1962, but Cardenas put pressure on Lopez Mateos on the peasant issue by forming a new *peon* party, the CCI (*Central Campesina Independiente*). The Lopez Mateos-Cardenas rift was then partially bridged by the creation of an executive post for Cardenas within the government.

In another reform in 1962, a constitutional amendment gave the government authority to require that business share their profits with their workers.

Riots & Leftist Activity

Leftist students rioted in Mexico City Aug. 9, 1960, and David Alfaro Siqueiros, recently elected secretary-general of the Mexican Communist Party, was arrested for allegedly organizing the riot. (He pleaded innocent to the charges Aug. 16.) The demonstrators, protesting the recent ouster of the leftist leaders of the city's Teachers Union, battled police with sticks and stones for 2 hours. 10 policemen and 11 rioters were injured; 43 persons were arrested. Siqueiros and left-wing journalist Filomeno Mata were sentenced to 8-year prison terms Mar. 10, 1962 for organizing the Aug. 1960 riot. 21 months was reduced from Siqueiros' term for time he had spent in jail awaiting trial and sentence, and he was pardoned by Lopez Mateos July 13, 1964 and freed.

A general strike by citizens of San Luis Potosi had been halted Dec. 9, 1959 by a truce arranged by the Lopez Mateos administration. The strike had been started Dec. 2 to force the dismissal of San Luis State Gov. Manuel Alvarez. It closed down the city's schools, factories and transportation system. Alvarez' ouster was demanded as a way of breaking the power of a political machine headed by Col. Gonzalo N. Santos, which had held absolute power over the state administration for 18 years. An election held Dec. 7 for mayor of the city of San Luis gave 26,319 votes to independent candidate Salvador Nava martiney to 1,683 for administration candidate Francisco Gutierrez Castellanos although Nava's name did not appear on ballots prepared by the Santos machine and voters were forced to paste Nava's name on the ballot with stickers supplied by the Potosina Civic Union. 3,000 Mexican Army troops occupied San Luis Potosi Dec. 6 to prevent election disorders. Violence had broken out Dec. 5 when a 6-year-old child and a secret service agent were shot by state policemen who fired into a crowd in front of the city jail demanding the release of 120 prisoners.

2d Secy. Nicolai M. Remisov and military attache Nicolai V. Aksenov of the Soviet embassy in Mexico City had been ordered Mar. 31, 1959 to leave Mexico because of their alleged involvement in a nationwide railroad strike called Mar. 25. It was charged that Demetrio Vallejo Martinez, secretary general of the Railroad Workers Union and an ex-Communist Party member, had been in frequent conferences with Remisov and Aksenov. Vallejo and 500 other alleged strike leaders were arrested Mar. 28. (The walkout had been called to support workers on 2 small lines who had gone on strike for a 16% wage increase.) Vallejo was kept in prison without trial until Sept. 1962 despite the constitutional limit of one year for such detention.

13 persons were killed and 37 wounded Dec. 30, 1960 when troops fired at 2,000 demonstrators protesting against the Guerrero state regime of Gov. Raul Caballero Aburto in Chilpancingo. The demonstrators, who demanded Caballero's resignation, charged him with corruption. (Caballero Aburto was dismissed as governor Jan. 4, 1961 after a federal government investigation of charges of corruption.)

224 alleged planners of Mexican street riots that were to start Sept. 15, 1961 were arrested Sept. 10 at the Mexico City suburban home of Gen. Celestino Gasca, 70, who had been linked to leftist labor movements. Gasca, in whose home police found arms and ammunition, was placed under house arrest. All but 6 of those arrested were reported released by Sept. 12. Constitution Revolutionary Party Pres. Mario Guerra Leal charged Sept. 12 that the alleged plot had been financed and directed by the Cuban government and its Mexican embassy. 29 of those arrested were indicted Sept. 26 on charges of crimes against the government, including homicide, attempted rebellion and making and carrying weapons. Among those indicted were Gen. Gasca and Dr. Salvador Nava Martinez, ex-San Luis Potosi mayor. Nava's unsuccessful candidacy in the San Luis Potosi state gubernatorial elections several months previously had precipitated anti-government riots by his followers. Several persons had been killed in recent anti-government riots there.

Soldiers at a Jatilpan military barracks Sept. 15, 1961 repulsed an attack by 200 persons armed with pistols and machetes. One soldier and one civilian were killed. 15 of the attackers were arrested, including the leader of the group, retired Col. Jenaro Coatla Gomez. Veracruz officials called the attack part of a widespread political military movement that authorities had sought to smash Sept. 14 with arrests in Veracruz and Pueblo states.

2,000 delegates attended a leftist-sponsored Latin American Conference for National Sovereignty, Economic Emancipation & Peace in Mexico City Mar. 5-8, 1961. Speeches attacking the U.S. were made at the Mar. 5 session by ex-Pres. Lazaro Cardenas and Alberto Y. Casella of Argentina, Cardenas, Casella and Domingo Vellasco of Brazil, co-sponsors of the conference and all directors of the Moscow-based World Peace Council, were elected conference presidents Mar. 6. Cardenas had charged at a Mexico City press interview Feb. 17 that Mexican newspapers had imposed a virtual "blackout" on coverage of the conference. Cardenas denied that the conference was being financed by Cuba's Castro regime. He said the money came from the "little people" of Mexico.

Economic Developments

The Mexican government purchased several foreign-owned utilities firms in 1960. Companies or company stocks were bought instead of being nationalized as in 1938. (The government in 1938 had also taken control of foreign companies, first expropriating them and then offering indemnities. Some indemnities were payed over a decade later.) The government bought the U.S. owned Impulsora de Empresas Electricas for about $70 million Apr. 26. The firm, a subsidiary of the American & Foreign Power Co., was the 2d largest privately operated electric manufacturing and distributing company in Mexico. The government took control of a majority of the Belgian-owned Mexican Light & Power Co. stock for $54 million (announced Sept. 1). The government bought Industrial Electrica Mexicana from the California Power Co. for $5.6 million (disclosed Sept. 12).

An improvement in the balance of trade took place in this period. The value of exports rose from $814 million in

1961 to $948 million in 1962, tourism produced an additional inflow of $755 million in the 2-year period, and the value of imports rose from $1.13 billion in 1961 to only $1.14 billion in 1962. The gross national product reached a value of $11.6 billion in 1962.

Agrarian Agitation & Reform

The Department of Agrarian Affairs announced a far-reaching program of land redistribution July 20, 1962. The agrarian reform plan called for distributing land to about 2 million small farmers over the next few years. It was the largest proposed land reform since the 1930s.

The government proposed to carry out a nationwide land survey financed by a $60 million U.S. agricultural loan. 2 types of *ejidal* land were to be distributed: (1) individually tilled communal farmland, and (2) cooperatively tilled farmland. About 53% of Mexican farmland is *ejidal*, a total of about 25 million acres.

In the individually tilled *ejidos,* fewer than 15% of the *campesinos* held title to their parcels. (The right to possess titles to land parcels is the major difference between the *ejido* and the Soviet *kholkhoz* or the Israeli *kibbutz*. Title to an *ejidal* land parcel does not carry the right to sell, lease or mortgage.) In the *ejidal* cooperatives (initiated by Lazaro Cardenas), the members are granted not land titles but guarantees of agrarian rights somewhat analogous to labor contracts.

Implementation of the land reforms dragged during 1962, although Lopez Mateos reported in his state-of-the-nation address Sept. 1, 1962 that 8,323,900 acres of land had been given to landless farmers during the preceding 12 months.

The announcement of the reforms sparked agitation and land revindications among various peasant groups.

Bands of *compesinos* began to invade and to squat on private property. Such *jacqueries* occurred in the states of Sinaloa, Sonora, Chihuahua, Coahuila and Durango. Federal troops were reported to have evicted 5,000 squatters along the Durango-Chihuahua border in early Jan. 1963. Intrusions on cattle ranches were reported in Casas Grandes (Chihuahua state). The invasions were said to have been directed mainly by the General Union of Laborers & Campesinos (farm-labor branch of the Marxist Popular Socialist Party) and the Central Campesino Independiente (new farm-labor grouping linked to the National Liberation Movement).

The controversial farm labor leader Ruben Jaramillo of the state of Morelos had been murdered in May 1962. Men purporting to be federal troops took Jaramillo, his wife and their 2 sons from their home, and the 4 were later found shot to death.

Ex-Pres. Cardenas had begun to form a new organization of landless peasants to pressure the government into implementing and expanding its agrarian reforms. Cardenas and other critics of the Lopez Mateos administration pointed out that the agrarian reform did not include the expropriation of foreigners' land holdings in Mexico.

Lopez Mateos had already tried to forestall trouble from Cardenas by creating a new council of ex-presidents to be incorporated into the government. The council, more or less tailored for Cardenas, would was to have an influential advisory role in the government. Each living ex-president was given an executive post as a project director or adviser. Cardenas became executive director of a major development project, the Balsas River Commission. (Other appointments: Miguel Aleman—chairman of the National Tourism Consultative Board; Abelardo L. Rodriguez—chairman of the Fisheries Bureau in the Commerce Department; Adolfo Ruiz Cortines—special adviser on non-metallic mineral resources; Emilio Portes Gil—chairman of the National Insurance Commission; Pascual Ortiz Rubio—government representative in the National Association of Engineers; Roque Gonsalez Garza*—coordinator of public works in Hidalgo state.)

Despite his incorporation into the government, Cardenas

---

*Gonsalez Garza (sometimes spelled Gonsales Garcia) had served briefly as president Jan. 16-June 11, 1915.

went ahead with plans for a new pressured grouping of landless peasants. The new organization was formed Jan. 7, 1963 during the 2d day of a 3-day congress in Mexico City. The organization, called the Farm Labor Independent Central (Central Campesina Independiente, or CCI), was opposed to the U.S. and the Lopez Mateos administration. The CCI's principal objective: to campaign for the break-up and distribution of large farms owned by foreigners. Speakers at the congress said that there were 3 million landless peasants in Mexico, that 197,600,000 acres of land were owned by 9,600 individuals and that only 50 million acres were under cultivation. CCI warned the administration that it would engage in nationwide demonstrations unless the government effected a more extensive land-distribution program.

Cardenas, who spoke at the opening of the CCI congress Jan. 6, said at a news conference later that the CCI had no formal connection with the left-wing National Liberation Movement (NLM). These 2 NLM leaders, however, attended the meeting; Cuahutemoc Cardenas, Cardenas' son, and Braulio Maldonado, ex-governor of the state of Baja (lower) California and one of the principal CCI organizers. Most of the CCI leaders were active in *campesino* affairs in the states of Baja California, Sonora and Neuva Leon and also in the states of Sinaloa, Chihuahua, Coahuila and Durango.

Secy. Gen. Vincente Lombardo Toledano of the (Marxist) Popular Socialist Party, in a statement issued Jan. 8, called the CCI "a dangerously divisive force" in the national *campesino* movement and asserted that its creation displayed "the hand of the Mexican Communist Party." Lombardo Toledano said the CCI and NLM were "playing along with the imperialist monopolists" by dividing the *campesino* movement.

Javier Rojo Gomez, director of the administration-sponsored National Campesino Federation, said Jan. 9 that the CCI was a "tempest in a tea pot" and would not affect federal land redistribution programs.

Ultimately, the CCI failed to become a major force in Mexican politics.

DIAZ ORDAZ ADMINISTRATION, 1964-70

The administration of Gustavo Diaz Ordaz appeared to be largely unconcerned with political and social reforms, concentrating instead on industrialization and economic improvement. The government often consulted Mexico's major business organizations, such as CONCANACO (Confederacion de Camaras Nacionales de Comercio) and CONCAMIN (Confederacion de Camaras Industriales), and was widely regarded as Mexico's most conservative government to date.

The Diaz Ordaz administration, however, claimed several significant social improvements. According to government figures, secondary school enrollment rose at least 20% during the 1962-70 period. UNESCO funds were used to create a large new Regional Technical Industrial Educational Center for technical training in Guadalajara. Continuing Lopez Mateos' 1962 land reform project, Diaz Ordaz redistributed 9 million hectares of land by May 1968, according to government figures.

The Diaz Ordaz period was one of continuing economic expansion. 20 new dams were built, 4 of them major sources for irrigation:

Name of Dam	River	New Hectares under Irrigation
Jose Maria Morelos ...	Rio Balsas	18,000
Vincente Guerio.	Rio Polivtla	18,000
Ignacio Allende	Rio de la Laja	12,600
Franciso Villa.	Rio Poanas.	5,000

Agricultural productivity improved markedly during this period, largely as a result of better seeds and improved irrigation.

The Mexican economy as a whole also grew steadily. The GNP (gross national product) grew from $15.68 billion in 1961 to $23.32 billion in 1967 (government figures). Over the same period the GNP per capita (average value earned

by each Mexican) grew from $426 to $510 (government estimates). Through the 1960s, however, the population grew at
a rate of about $3\frac{1}{2}\%$ a year, thus absorbing about half of
Mexico's economic gains.

Mexico's dependence on foreign trade decreased during
the Diaz Ordaz administration, but its balance of payments
deficit rose steeply. Government economists attributed this
rise largely to the lack of diversification in exports. This
lack exposed the nation to sharp seasonal drops in foreign
earnings as a result of crop failures and bad weather.

The 1968 Mexico City Olympic Games attracted world
attention and helped to build Mexico's tourist industry. National earnings from tourism have increased about 13% since
the games were held.

The most serious civil disorders in postwar Mexico took
place during Diaz Ordaz administration. A number of persons were killed and seriously wounded during student anti-
government demonstrations in Aug. 1968. The demonstrations were regarded as a puerile disorder by conservatives, but
liberals called them a rebirth of the struggle for civil liberties.

Gustavo Diaz Ordaz was born in 1909 in the state of
Puebla. He was trained as a lawyer and became professor of
administrative law at Puebla University, a Roman Catholic
institution. After serving in the Chamber of Deputies he became a senator for Puebla State. The newly elected Ruiz
Cortines appointed him in 1952 as head of legal affairs in
the Interior Ministry *(gobernacion)*, and he soon became head
of the department. He was appointed minister of the interior
by Lopez Mateos in 1958, and he resigned from the cabinet
at the end of 1963 to run for the presidency.

Diaz Ordaz Elected President

Gustavo Diaz Ordaz, 53, was elected president of Mexico
July 5, 1964. The ruling Institutional Revolutionary Party
(PRI) claimed July 6 that about 90% of the votes cast in the
general elections had gone to its presidential candidate, Diaz
Ordaz, and to its candidates for the Senate and Chamber of

Deputies. Diaz Ordaz was opposed by Jose Gonzalez Torres, the candidate of the rightist PAN *(Partido de Accion Nacional)*.

The official results certified in September showed that Diaz Ordaz had won 8.4 million votes and Gonzalez Torres nearly a million. Slightly fewer than 31,000 votes were cast for write-in candidates. Out of a registered electorate of 13,589.000, $9\frac{1}{2}$ million Mexican citizens voted.

In the congressional elections, all 60 senators elected were PRI candidates. Among them were Mexico's first women senators, Maria Lavalle Urbina (Campeche state) and Alicia Tapia Arellano (Sonora state). Of the 210 deputies elected to the Chamber of Deputies, 175 represented the PRI, 20 represented the right-wing Catholic PAN, 10 the *Partido Popular Socialista* (PRS) and 5 the *Partido Autentica de la Revolucion Mexicana* (PARM).

The *Partido Popular Socialista* was an updated version of Vicente Lombardo Toledano's *Partido Popular*. The *Partido Popular* had faded as a militant opposition party after the Lombardo Toledano-Ruiz Cortines reconciliation early in 1953. The PPS supported the PRI presidential candidates both in 1958 and in 1964.

The *Partido Autentica de la Revolucion Mexicana* was created prior to the 1961 congressional elections, in which it won 2% of the vote. It was composed of elderly revolutionaries who believed that the authentic Mexican revolution had been betrayed. The PARM made little effort to win elections, partly because of the age of many of its members and partly because it saw itself largely as a symbol or rallying-point.

Diaz Ordaz, 53, was inaugurated for his 6-year term as president Dec. 1, 1964. He promised in his inaugural address that his administration would take forceful action to improve the lot of the farm workers. Diaz Ordaz said: "6 million Mexicans, or half the national labor force, work in the countryside. For their benefit we will bring to bear the greatest forces of agrarian reform, we will accelerate the distribution of land. . . . The country has contributed much without reserve to the basic development of industry, and now industry must

contribute to the solution of the rural problems. . . . Direct
investment coming from abroad can play an important part
in accelerating economic progress, and it is always welcome
as long as it is subject to our laws . . . and contributes to the
social objectives of our country. . . . Labor's own conscience
must reaffirm that union rights be exercised responsibly and
for the enforcement, betterment and solidarity guaranteed to
unionism under the law."

Diaz Ordaz chose a cabinet that included several signifi-
cant holdovers. Remaining in the cabinet from the regime of
Pres. Adolfo Lopez Mateos were: *Minister of Government (and
Interior)*—Luis Echeverria Alvarez;   *Treasury (and Finance &
Public Credit)*—Antonio Ortiz Mena;   *Labor & Social Welfare*
—Salomon Gonzalez Blanco;   *Regent of the Federal District*—
Ernesto P. Uruchurtu. The following men, all of whom had
worked their way up in the ranks of the PRI "machine,"
completed the new cabinet: *Foreign Relations*—Antonio Car-
rillo Flores (appointed 1964); *Industry & Commerce*—Octa-
viano Campos Salas (appointed 1964); *National Defense*—
Marcelino Garcia Barragan (appointed 1964); *Agriculture*—
Juan Gil Preciado (appointed 1966); *Communications & Transport*—Jose Antonio Padilla Seguro; *Regent of the Federal District*—Alfonso Corona del Rosal (appointed 1966); *Attorney
General*—Julio Sanchez Vargas (appointed 1968).

(Congressional elections were again held in 1967. The
PRI July 2, 1967 won all 178 contested seats in the 210-
member Chamber of Deputies. The PRI won 87% of the vote
and the National Action Party [PAN] 8%; the remainder
was largely shared by the *Partido Popular Socialista* and the
PARM. The PRI captured all 7 state governorships but lost
to PAN in several municipal elections in Sonora state).

RELATIONS WITH THE U.S.

Relations between Mexico and the U.S. were largely
untroubled during the Diaz Ordaz administration. The 2 nations made headway in resolving 2 outstanding questions:
Colorado River over-salinity and off-shore fishing rights. The

2 nations also signed a treaty ending a long-standing border dispute caused by changes in the Rio Grande river bed.

Perhaps the greatest damage to U.S.-Mexican relations in this period was the U.S. military intervention in the Dominican Republic in Apr. 1965. Many observers held that the image of the U.S. was tarnished in Mexican eyes by this act reminiscent of the days of "gunboat diplomacy." The U.S. move was condemned by the otherwise pro-U.S. Pres. Gustavo Diaz Ordaz.

U.S. Intervention in Dominican Republic

The Dominican Republic on the Caribbean island of Hispanola had been ruled by the dictator Rafael Leonidas Trujillo from 1930 until his assassination May 31, 1961. With the election of Juan Bosch Dec. 20, 1962, as the first con-stitutionallv chosen president of the Dominican Republic since 1924, there was considerable hope that peaceful, demo-cratic government had finally been established. But charges of Communist sympathy were leveled at Bosch, and finally disagreements with the armed forces led to his ouster by the military in Sept. 1963. Bosch, exiled in Puerto Rico, called for the return of the 1963 constitution and predicted strong opposition within the Dominican Republic to the new civilian regime that replaced the military junta. Meanwhile, Donald Joseph Reid Cabral emerged as the head of a new civilian junta and through late 1964 and early 1965 apparently at-tempted to lessen the power of the armed forces and bring them under civilian control. In response to U.S. pressures, the junta set elections for the summer of 1965 and later re-vised this date to September of that year.

Reid Cabral's civilian triumvirate was overthrown Apr. 24, 1965 in an armed *coup d'etat* by army rebels seeking to re-install Juan Bosch. Air force and navy elements opposed to Bosch's return resisted the army insurgents, who were as-sisted by pro-Bosch civilians, and fierce fighting between the opposing military forces erupted Santo Domingo.

A contingent of 405 U.S. Marines landed in Santo

Domingo by helicopter Apr. 28, ostensibly to protect and evacuate American civilians endagered by the civil strife. This was the first time since 1928 that American Marines had made a landing in a Latin American country. In a statement issued May 1, the U.S. State Department denied that American troops in the Dominican Republic were taking sides in the conflict. "But before that statement could be published in any newspaper," the *Washington Post* noted May 2, "an American admiral was being quoted as saying that U.S. forces were in the Dominican Republic for the dual purpose of saving American lives and 'seeing that Castro and Cuban Communists do not get in.'"

At their May 1 meeting, following the U.S. action, the OAS foreign ministers approved without dissent a Mexican resolution establishing a 5-man OAS peace commission to help restore order in the Dominican Republic. The U.S.' military involvement came under attack May 1 by the delegates of Mexico, Venezuela and Chile. Raphael de la Colina of Mexico called on the foreign ministers' council to adopt a statement expressing "deep concern, surprise and consternation at such unilateral acts." According to the London *Observer*, "what is unprecedented . . . is the unanimous condemnation of U.S. intervention by the governments of Latin America, whatever their political complexion, with Mexico and Chile in the lead." Mexican and other Latin American criticism seemed to center about an alleged U.S. violation of Article 17 of the OAS Charter, which said: "The territory of a state is inviolable; it may not be the object, even temporarily, of military occupation or of other measures of force taken by another state, directly or indirectly, under any grounds whatever."

Nevertheless the OAS foreign ministers May 6 approved by 14-5 vote (Venezuela abstaining) a U.S. resolution to establish an Inter-American Armed Force to guarantee the cease-fire arrangement and help restore order in the Dominican Republic. The 5 dissenting votes were cast by Mexico, Uruguay, Chile, Ecuador and Peru. (Supporting the resolution were: the U.S., the Dominican Republic, Argentina, Bolivia, Brazil,

Colombia, Costa Rica, Haiti, Honduras, Nicaragua, Panama, Paraguay and El Salvador.) (The force formally started its peace-keeping operations in Santo Domingo May 23.)

The OAS ministers May 10, by 14-3 vote, approved a Costa Rican resolution extending the mandate of the OAS peace commission. The resolution was opposed by Mexico, Chile and Uruguay, Venezuela, Ecuador and Peru abstained.

Pres. Diaz Ordaz, at a joint session of Congress in Mexico City Sept. 1, stated his disapproval of the U.S.' intervention in the Dominican Republic. He urged that relations between Mexico and its "immediate neighbors" serve as "an example of cordial and constructive co-existence."

Disputes Resolved

Several Mexican-U.S. problems were resolved during the Diaz Ordaz administration:

Foreign Min. Antonio Carrillo Flores announced Jan. 13, 1965 that he and U.S. negotiators had agreed on a plan to reduce the salt content of irrigation waters flowing from the Colorado River in the U.S. to Mexico. Farmers in Mexico had complained since 1962 (when the U.S. started a reclamation project in the Colorado River area of Arizona) that excessive salt in irrigation waters was damaging their crops in the Mexicai valley.

Mexico and the U.S. agreed to implement a fishing agreement granting "reciprocal privileges to U.S. and Mexican fishermen in waters between 9 and 12 nautical miles off each other's coasts for 5 years commencing Jan. 1, 1968." The agreement was reached in Oct. 1967, and details were worked out at a Jan. 4, 1968 meeting of the International Boundary & Water Commission in El Paso. Tex.

Diaz Ordaz met with U.S. Pres. Richard M. Nixon (inaugurated Jan. 20, 1969) in the Mexican Pacific coastal resort of Puerto Vallarta Apr. 20-1, 1970. The 2 heads of state agreed on a treaty settling the long-standing border dispute caused by changes in the Rio Grande river bed. The border agreement had been worked out beforehand in talks between

Mexican Foreign Min. Carrillo Flores and U.S. State Secy.
William P. Rogers. The treaty was ratified by the U.S. Senate
Nov. 29, 1971 and by the Mexican Senate Dec. 30, 1971.

The instruments of ratification were exchanged Apr. 18,
1972 in a ceremony at the U.S. State Department in Washington. The comprehensive treaty formally incorporated the
principles approved by Nixon and Diaz Ordaz. A State
Department press release explained the treaty terms in
detail:

First, the 2 governments agree on the settlement of all existing territorial differences, including a major dispute,outstanding since 1907, over a part
of the Presidio-Ojinaga Valley, about 200 miles southeast of El Paso, Texas.
Approximately 1,606 acres in the Presidio-Ojinaga Valley will be recognized
as subject to Mexican sovereignty while about 555 acres of the disputed
tracts are retained by the United States. Some 252 acres will be transferred
to the United States by Mexico elsewhere in the Presidio-Ojinaga Valley in
recognition of the number [182] of small islands passing to Mexico in a re-
sortation of the boundary to the middle of the Rio Grande. In the Lower
Rio Grande Valley equal parcels of about 481 acres will be exchanged
between the 2 countries. The course of the Rio Grande will be relocated in
these areas to place all U.S. territory north of the river and all Mexican territory south of the river.

2d, the 2 governments agree to the restoration and maintenance of the
Rio Grande and Colorado River as continuous natural boundaries. . . . Incorporated in the treaty are procedures to guard against future loss of territory by either country; that is, when a river changes its channel and shifts
a land tract not exceeding 617.76 acres and no more than 100 inhabitants from
one side of the river to the other, the country from which it was separated
has the right to restore the river to its original channel within 3 years (with
a possible one-year extension). If the restoration is not performed, sovereignty passes to the country to which the land has become attached, and the
"losing" national will be entitled to receive later compensation of an equal
arèa in another natural separation or in a future rectification in the boundary
section of the river. In cases of larger tracts or population, the 2 governments will jointly restore or rectify the river, again maintaining the river
boundary.

3d, the treaty establishes maritime boundaries between the United States
and Mexico in the Pacific Ocean and the Gulf of Mexico. These lines will be
based on the equidistance principle adopted in the 1958 Geneva Convention
on the Territorial Sea and the Contiguous Zone but will be partially
straightened for ease of determination and demarcation. They will be drawn
to a distance of 12 nautical miles from the coasts without prejudice to the
position of either Government as to the extent of internal waters, of the
territorial sea, or of sovereign rights or jurisdiction for any other purpose.
Because of the lateral migration of the mouth of the Rio Grande caused
by ocean current in the Gulf of Mexico, a short segment of the maritime
boundary will swing with the mouth of the river, running from a fixed

point 2,000 feet off the present mouth, to the mouth of the river wherever it may be at any future time.

(The somewhat analogous Chamizal dispute, which had been resolved during the Lopez Mateos-Kennedy talks in June 1962, had been formally ended Oct. 28, 1967, when Diaz Ordaz met briefly with U.S. Pres. Lyndon Baines Johnson for ceremony at Ciudad Juarez during which the Chamizal Territory was legally transferred to Mexico.)

Other Developments

The Mexican government continued to demand greater Mexican control of foreign companies doing business in Mexico. In response to these demands, a subsidiary of the General Electric Co., General Electric de Mexico, S.A., put 10% of its stock on public sale to Mexicans July 1, 1968. The move was regarded as a major success in the government's demand for Mexican equity in all foreign firms. General Electric de Mexico had long resisted selling any shares to Mexicans; Ford, General Motors and hundreds of other foreign companies in Mexico continued to operate without any Mexican capital participation. In what was described as the most important nationalization act of the Diaz Ordaz administration, the government-owned oil firm Pemex took over prospecting rights that had been granted to 4 U.S. oil companies in 1949-51, the *Journal of Commerce* reported June 9, 1969. The cancellation of the firms' contracts involved payment of $18 million to the 4 companies—Continental Oil, Pauley Petroleum, Pauley Pan American Petroleum and American Independent Oil—and the return to Mexico of exclusive rights to explore drill and exploit oil resources along its Gulf coast.

U.S. Pres. Richard M. Nixon sent New York State Gov. Nelson A. Rockefeller on fact-finding missions to Mexico and other Latin-American countries in 1969. The Mexican mission was regarded as an attempt to widen business and trade contacts between the U.S. and Mexico. Rockefeller spent 11 days in Mexico and other Central American republics

in May. In his report to Nixon Nov. 9, 1969, Rockefeller
emphasized that an anti-U.S. trend was sweeping Central
America. All the American nations were "a tempting target
for communism," Rockefeller said.

ECONOMIC GROWTH & DOMESTIC UNREST

The years of the Diaz Ordaz administration were generally considered as perhaps the most conservative period in
the history of Mexico's PRI-dominated government.

The Diaz government was said to have sacrificed a good
deal of the traditional populist appeal of the PRI. In its
attempt to build up the national economy, it was held, the
government tended to slight working-class and opposition
groups that could hamper the economic freedom of business
management interests. The government apparently acted on
the assumption that Mexican commerce and industry could not
compete with the powerful U.S. businesses active in Mexico if
their hands were tied by strikes or left-wing opposition.

The most severe opposition to the government surfaced
as civil disturbances in Mexico City, during July-Oct. 1968.
Although the leaders of the anti-government demonstrations
were mostly students and other intellectuals of middle-class
origin, they served to awaken other social groups to the idea
that their interests were no longer being served by the increasingly business-dominated PRI government.

Militant Dissidence Grows

The Mexican Communist Party (PCM) continued to
function legally during the Diaz Ordaz administration but as
an unregistered organization not entitled to run candidates
for office in national elections, Its membership was estimated
at about 5,000 in 1968, but it had considerable influence in
the Central Campesino Independiente (CCI), a peasant pressure group, and in student groups.

Other extreme left-wing groups were the Popular Electoral Front and an elusive new Maoist Communist group.

The Popular Electoral Front was a coalition of Communists and members of the CCI. It was led by revolutionary ex-Pres. Lazaro Cardenas, founder of the CCI. The Popular Electoral Front had intended to sponsor a presidential candidate in 1964 but at the last moment reached an agreement with Diaz Ordaz and shifted its support to his candidacy.

Members of both the PCM (pro-Moscow) and of Maoist Communist groups were arrested on conspiracy charges during the Diaz Ordaz period. Among major arrests:

• PCM Secy. Gen. Manuel Terrazas Guerrero and associate editor Hugo Ponce de Leon of *La Voz de Mexico,* the official PCM organ, were among 30 Communists and leftists arrested Apr. 13-14, 1965 for alleged conspiracy against the government.

• The Mexican government announced July 19, 1967 that it had discovered an alleged conspiracy to overthrow the PRI government and replace it with a "people's Socialist regime based on the thought of Mao Tse-tung." 13 persons were arrested, including a Venezuelan and a Salvadorean. The government claimed that the alleged conspirators planned to train guerrilla terrorists in the jungles of Chiapas State in southern Mexico. The alleged conspirators were accused of preparing illegal actions in Mexico City and elsewhere and of having already dynamited an army truck in Guerrero State in an attempt to seize arms by force. The Mexican attorney general's department claimed that the Mexican office of Hsinhua (mainland China's New China News Agency) was financing the conspiracy with $1,680 a month. The department alleged that Javier Fuentes Gutierrez, a civil engineer and former PCM member, was the conspiracy's ringleader. The arrested Salvadorean, Silvestre Enrique Marenco Martinez, was identified as a veteran of left-wing guerrilla campaigns in Nicaragua.

• Mario Renato Menendez Rodriquez, publisher of the leftist magazine *Por Que,* was arrested Feb. 12, 1970 and charged Feb. 14 with financing guerrilla training camps in Tabasco and Chiapas states and with masterminding a number of terrorist bombings in Mexico City. 6 other persons were also arrested in connection with the charges.

Other cases of violent dissidence involved agricultural laborers, intellectuals and students:

• Violence erupted in Guerrero state when a wildcat faction of a coconut growers' union attacked participants at a meeting Aug. 20,1967 between coconut producers and representatives of the rival faction of the union. About 700 members of the rival union factions waged a 20-minute gunfight in which 23 persons were shot dead and nearly 100 wounded.

Mexican authorities said Aug. 21 that the fighting had erupted when some 1500 farmers armed with pistols and machine guns and led by Cesar del Angel, the Veracruz representative in the Federal Chamber of Deputies, tried to enter a meeting of the Regional Copra Producers Union in Acapulco and fired into the building when they were refused admittance. The members inside the building, also armed, immediately returned the fire. Police and army units finally restored order, arrested 183 people and confiscated a cache of arms in the building. Although wounded, del Angel was reported to have escaped. Guerrero Gov. Raimondo Abarca Alarcon charged Aug. 21 that del Angel was responsible for the killings and ordered his detention. Del Angel, in a statement appearing Aug. 22 in the newspaper *Ultimas Noticias,* charged that state policemen and paid gunmen were responsible for attacking the union building. He blamed Abarca for the gun battle.

• Troops took control of the city of Durango Jan. 20, 1970 in the face of strikes and demonstrations against the state government. A 2-day student sit-in at the Cerro del Mercado mining firm had been followed by a general sit-in. In addition, the city had been plagued with a university strike and a merchants' work stoppage.

Mexico City Riots of 1968

The most violent civil disorders in postwar Mexican history took place in Mexico City in the summer and autumn of 1968. The occasion for the disorders, which took the form of street fighting and rioting with a high number of dead and wounded, was a 4-month strike by Mexico City university and high-school students. The striking students were opposed by government armed forces consisting mainly of riot police (*granaderos*) and, for a period, of military troops supported by light armor. The government was reported to have been worried that the demonstrations might seriously disrupt the 1968 summer Olympics, which ultimately took place as scheduled in Mexico City in Oct. 1968.

The civil disorders had several dimensions:

(1) University and high-school life in the capital was totally disrupted for the entire period. The academic community emerged from the disruptions shaken and uncertain: there were pleas for reform of the entire structure of higher education in Mexico.

(2) The riots were part of an international wave of student discontent in 1968. Many countries were affected by student riots and demonstrations that year, including Egypt, France, Italy, the U.S. and Yugoslavia. Serious disorders involving students in France and the U.S. had been reported in Mexico before the Mexico City strife began.

(3) The struggle between the students and the PRI-dominated government inevitably attracted into the fray opponents of the PRI. In this way the student protests became a focus of general protest by many citizens who were discontented with the PRI for various reasons. Since the PRI had become predominantly conservative and business-oriented by 1968, anti-government demonstrators were frequently radicals and left-wingers. However, many other people, small businessmen, workers, Catholics, intellectuals, joined the anti-government demonstrations.

The incidents causing the outbreak of the student strike, which eventually came to involve more than 150,000 of the capital's students, were never made fully known. The trouble may have started with police interference in a brawl between rival city high schools. Student rioting had gradually begun to erupt all over the city by the end of July, with demonstrators using gutted cars and buses as barricades to resist the

onslaught of riot police and infantry. Tension mounted July
28-9, and by July 30 there was a virtual battle in which 3,000
students in the city center attacked tanks and half-tracks
with Molotov cocktails and cobblestones. About 60 students
and 25 policemen were injured. There were no officially confirmed deaths.

The demonstrations reached a climax when troops used
a bazooka to blow down the door of a high school July 30.
Since Mexico City high schools form an ancillary part of the
National University, much of the academic community was
outraged at this extreme violation of the principle of university autonomy legally guaranteed and hitherto traditionally
honored in Mexico City. By July 31 every institution of
higher learning and every secondary school in the capital
had been closed for one reason or another. Students occupied
the premises of National University, the National Polytechnic
Institute and other institutions of learning.

Student unrest continued in Mexico City, with demonstrations in the center of the city Aug. 13 and 27 and a clash
between students and police in front of the National Palace
Aug. 28. A student strike, affecting some 87,200 students at
the National University and 62,700 at the National Poly-
technical Institute, began Aug. 9. Student leaders said the
strike and demonstrations had been launched to support a
list of demands presented to the government. These demands
included: (1) The freeing of all political prisoners in Mexico;
(2) abrogation of Article 145 of the Penal Code, which gave
the government power to punish acts of subversion, treason
and public disorder under the general heading of "social
dissolution"; (3) elimination of the special riot police; (4) the
ouster of Mexico City Police Chief Luis Cueto and his
deputy; (5) the paying of indemnities to victims of the clashes
with police July 26 and 30, when troops occupied the National University campus; and (6) the guarantee of university
autonomy.

The August demonstrations were noted for their animo-
sity toward Pres. Gustavo Diaz Ordaz. The president had not
yet been personally criticized. In his 4th annual report to the

nation, Diaz Ordaz said Sept. 1 that he would not allow the students to disrupt the opening of Olympic Games. But he offered the students "first steps" toward meeting of their demands, including a pledge to uphold university autonomy. He denied that there were political prisoners in Mexico and affirmed that all prisoners were serving terms for crimes they had committed. He said that some prisoners might be released, however, if pressure tactics were halted. He also proposed that the Penal Code be studied, perhaps by congressional public hearings. But the government Sept. 6 rejected the students' demand for the elimination of the riot police.

The *N.Y. Times* gave this description of the atmosphere in the capital Sept. 8: " . . . [The students] have plastered the walls and bulletin boards [of the National University] with revolutionary mottoes. In the School of Economics, quotations from Mao Tse-tung are seen. . . . The auditorium of the School of Philosophy and Letters has been renamed 'Auditorium Ernesto Che Guevara,' and classroom doors have been painted with such names as 'Lenin Room' or 'Ho Chi Minh Room.' Schools all over the city have taken on a revolutionary look, with students manning them 24 hours a day against possible intrusion by Government forces. . . . The [student] strike committee has no fixed meeting place, and its members are reluctant to have their pictures taken for fear of reprisals. Every political student organization is involved—Moscow Communists, Mao Communists, Castro Communists and Trotsky Communists. . . . From almost all the students come expressions denoting great lack of respect for governing officials, the Institutional Revolutionary Party [PRI], which has ruled under various names for almost 40 years, and all other political groups. . . . [The] bulk of the student body come[s] from the middle and upper classes, the peasant and industrial working classes rarely being represented."

The Mexican army seized control of the National University and evicted students from its buildings Sept. 18. Hundreds of students and some teachers were arrested, but most members of the National Strike Committee, an amorphous body of about 200 members eluded arrest. A statement by the Interior Ministry said that the government was fulfilling its obligation to preseve "juridical order in the entire national territory, of which the university is also an integral part."

Rioting was renewed Sept. 21-24 in the Tlatelolco district near the Foreign Ministry. Even more severe fighting also took place near the National Polytechnic Institute in the northwest part of the capital, where students for the first time opened fire on the police. Here a number of persons were killed (between 3 and 15, according to different accounts). Again many students were arrested.

The rector of the National University, Banos Sierra, announced his resignation Sept. 22, protesting against the breach of the university's autonomy. He withdrew his resignation Sept. 26, however, apparently after having reached an agreement for the evacuation of the National University campus. The 1,300 troops who had occupied the campus since Sept. 18 withdrew Sept. 30-Oct. 1 along with their tanks and armored cars.

After a lull of several days, during which social peace had apparently been restored, the worst fighting of the entire student strike erupted the evening of Oct. 2 on the central plaza of the Nonoalco-Tlatelolco housing project. Accounts differ on the actual events of the battle and the responsibility for its severity and high number of dead and wounded. Because of what took place then, however, the night of Oct. 2-3, 1968 is known in Mexico as *la noche triste,* or "the night of sorrow."

The trouble began when several thousand students gathered to begin a protest march against the continued occupation of the National Polytechnic Institute by government troops. A large number of non-students were also present at the rally, including many women and children. (Government accounts claimed that these non-students many of whom were later killed or wounded, were bystanders whose presence among the demonstrators went undetected; reports critical of the government alleged that these persons were sympathizers of the students—academics, merchants, working people, etc. —

whose presence at the rally was fully known to the governments troops.)

According to the government, the troops opened fire when snipers began shooting at them from nearby apartment buildings. However, the correspondent of the *N.Y. Times* claimed that the troops had simply opened fire on "what had been a peaceful student rally in the plaza." Students and their sympathizers called the event a "massacre," and it is frequently referred to in Mexico as the "Tlatelolco massacre." As the fighting continued, many noncombatants were caught in the crossfire. Government reports listed 28 dead and 200 wounded from gunfire during *la noche triste;* the correspondent of the *N.Y. Times,* however, said that it was "virtually certain" that at least 49 persons had been killed and 500 wounded. (Later estimates in the U.S. press ran much higher.) More than 1,000 students were arrested.

Agreement was reached to end the student strike Oct. 8, only 4 days before the official opening day of the Mexico City Olympic Games. Many arrested students were released in exchange for a student pledge that the strikers would not interfere with the Olympic Games. The Games took place without disruption, and the strike was formally ended Nov. 22. Many political prisoners, mostly stundents, remained under continued detention at the Lecumberri street prison in Mexico City.

An interpretation from the "liberal" point of view of the events leading up to the Tlatelolco tragedy was given by John Womack Jr. in 1970 in an article entitled "The Spoils of the Mexican Revolution" in the July 1970 issue of *Foreign Affairs:*

. . . Reported abroad as a student riot, described officially as a seditious conspiracy, this was at heart a civic movement for civil liberties. It had no particular martyr, champion, hero, boss, chief, sponsor or organization, only the solidarity of indignant citizens. Starting in Mexico City as a student defense of the universities against police intervention, it quickly matured into an offensive campaign of wide popular appeal against the government. . . . Not only students but also their parents, their teachers and many tens of thousands of office workers, housewives, shop workers, professionals and petty merchants marched in massive demonstrations to protest official abuse of civil rights. Militants demanded revocation of 2 articles in the Penal Code . . . which provide a sentence of 2 to 12 years for anyone convicted of spreading ideas that "tend to produce rebellion, sedition, riot or insurrection"

Ordinary demonstrators demanded simply that the constitution have the respect of men sworn to respect it. Out of the uproar the forbidden question came clear—If Mexico could afford the Olympics, could it not afford free politics? But the answer remained no, because free politics would introduce strategic risks that the nation's entrepreneurs would not admit—in an open regime their American rivals could press harder for advantages, while their native critics could press harder for redistribution of income, or even structural reforms. These dangers the government recognized in denouncing the demonstrators as tools of the CIA [the U.S.' Central Intelligence Agency] and the Communists. All summer long in 1968 it tried to contain them, politically and forcibly. In a crisis just before the Olympics it had to crush the movement. And on the rainy evening of Oct. 2, in Tlatelolco Plaza in Mexico City, the army surrounded a rally of 10,000 and machine-gunned the crowd, killing probably 50, wounding probably 1,000, arresting 1,500.

Official harassment still countinues. Since the Tlatelolco massacre at least 5 small rallies of the movement in Mexico City have been violently dispersed. A few student leaders have been suspiciously murdered. Many others have gone into hiding, and at least 3 have gove into political exile . . . . The poor souls that the police have in jail suffer special persecutions. When 81 of them in the Lecumberri Street prison in Mexico City carried on a hunger strike last winter, to protest their detention for more than a year without bail or trial, the warden had other inmates assault them. . . .

(Accounts of the condition of the Lecumberri prisoners were unreliable. The conclusion Jan. 20, 1970 of a 40-day hunger strike was widely reported in the foreign press. The main purpose of the hunger strike was to publicize the prisoners' situation. The Mexican government claimed to have released all prisoners by late 1972.)

Catholic Problems

Despite increasing government acceptance of the reality of Roman Catholicism in Mexican life, the Catholic political movement (PAN) did not gain significant strength during the Diaz Ordaz administration.

Representing the church, much of big business and certain upper and middle class professional people, the PAN *(Partido de Accion Nacional)* has been able to win only 8% to 10% of the vote. In the congressional elections of July 2, 1967 the PAN received 8% of the vote. On the basis of the proportional system, the PAN elected 20 deputies in 1967, the same number it had won in 1964.

One of the Catholic Church's major problems in Mexico

is the unpopular Vatican stance on birth control. Mexico, a nation plagued by chronic poverty, especially in rural areas where the church is strongest, had a population growth rate in 1970 of 3.4%, one of the higher rates in the Western Hemisphere.

Many Mexican Catholics have expressed the desire to see the Vatican's stance on birth control softened. The Church's traditional prohibition on birth control by artificial means, however, was reaffirmed in Pope Paul VI's encyclical *Humanae Vitae (Of Human Life),* made public by the Vatican July 29, 1968. (The encyclical, dated July 25, was written at the conclusion of 5 years of Vatican study of the issue.)

Previously, Mexican national opinion polls had indicated heavy opposition within the Catholic Church to the pope's birth-control ban. A letter sent by the Vatican to world Catholic leaders a week before the publication of the encyclical indicated that the pope had expected "bitterness" in response to the encyclical, and it called for a united front by bishops, priests and Catholic organizations to expound the teaching.

Mexico's 77 Roman Catholic archbishops and bishops, ending an annual meeting in Mexico City Aug. 10, 1968, indorsed the encyclical as "a solemn confirmation of a constant teaching of the [church] authority." (According to the unofficial Foundation for the Study of Population, Mexico had 600,000 known abortions annually, and about 32,000 women died each year there as a result of abortions. Dr. Luis Lenero, director of the Mexican Institute of Social Studies, said there was one abortion for every 8 live births in Mexico, it was reported April 9, 1969. Lenero blamed the high abortion rate on ignorance of birth control methods.)

Another much-debated issue in the worldwide Roman Catholic Church was that of sacerdotal celibacy, the ban on priestly marriage. A Mexican bishops' conference adopted a position favoring celibacy, *Le Monde* reported Jan. 20, 1969.

In another controversy between church liberals and conservatives, the Vatican Congregation for the Doctrine of the Faith issued an order forbidding Roman Catholic priests and nuns to participate in the activities of the Center for Intercultural Documentation (CIDOC) in Cuernavaca, Mexico, the center's director, Msgr. Ivan Illich, revealed Jan. 22, 1969. The action, which drew protests in a number of circles, resulted in Illich's "irrevocable" resignation from church service (disclosed Mar. 29). The Cuernavaca center had been established in 1961 to promote language studies and cultural contacts between religious leaders and Latin Americans. Though it had no official connection with the Catholic church, a large percentage of the students were priests or members of Catholic religious orders, and it had often served as an informed meeting ground for clergy and scholars interested in social change in Latin America. Illich, a priest of the Archdiocese of New York, was known as an advocate of church reform and of social action in Latin America. The Vatican attack, made in a letter from the head of the Congregation for the Doctrine of the Faith, Franjo Cardinal Seper, to the bishop of Cuernavaca, the Most Rev. Sergio Mendez Arceo (known as a supporter of the center), contained no specific charges. However, it asserted that "many complaints have been brought to the Holy See regarding the unfortunate effects that the instruction given in the aforesaid center brings about."

(Pope Paul VI Mar. 29, 1969 named 33 new cardinals including Miguel Dario Miranda y Gomez, 73, the archbishop of Mexico City.)

Economic Progress

Mexico experienced rapid economic growth in the late 1960s. Whereas in 1967 Latin America as a whole had failed to achieve the $2\frac{1}{2}\%$ increase in per capita gross national product set as a goal by the Alliance for Progress, the Alliance's Inter-American Committee (CIAP) reported Jan. 23, 1968 that Mexico had achieved an increase of 3.8%. While the 18 Alliance members had an estimated GNP increase of $4\frac{1}{2}\%$ in 1967, their average per capita GNP growth was only 1.6%. (Per capita GNP growth is GNP growth divided by a population increase coefficient.)

1968 was a particularly good year for economic growth in Mexico. This growth was partially a result of the Mexico City Olympic Games and partially a reflection of an ongoing business boom. The May issue of the *BOLSA* (Bank of London and South America) *Review* reported the following 1968 economic statistics: Exports in 1968 rose by 6.7% to $1.178 billion, but a 12.1% increase in the year's imports resulted in a $782 million trade deficit, about $138 million larger than 1967's deficit. However, this visible trade deficit was covered by net tourism receipts (which increased by 15½% to $510 million in 1968) and increased income from border transactions and direct foreign investment. Mexico's overall balance of payments showed a surplus of $49 million. The gross national product increased by 7.1% in 1968, compared with 6.4% in 1967. Per capita income increased by 3.4%, as against 2.7% in 1967.

The 1968 summer Olympics were credited by government economists with producing a major increase in national earnings from tourism. (Mexican tourism is an important means of offsetting the national trade deficit.) Latin America's first Olympics (and the first in the Americas since 1932) were held in Mexico City Oct. 21-27. 7,226 athletes from a record 119 nations competed in 19 events. The U.S., with a total of 107 medals, emerged as winner of the Games. The USSR, with 91 medals, was 2d. The U.S. won 45 gold medals (for first place), the USSR 29. The Games of the 19th Olympiad were officially opened Oct. 12 when a flame bowl was lit with the Olympic Torch carried into Olympic Stadium by Norma Enriqueta Basilio Sotelo, 20, a Mexican hurdler. She was the first woman in modern times to be given the honor. (The torch had been lit Aug. 23 in Olympia, Greece and had been relayed to Mexico City by ship and about 3,000 runners and 17 swimmers.) Mexico placed 16th in the games, winning 3 gold medals, 3 silver medals and 3 bronze medals.

Major economic events in Mexico during the Diaz Ordaz period included a redistribution of grazing land to peasants, an IBRD (International Bank for Reconstruction & Development, or World Bank) 5-year credit program for agricultural development and another large IBRD program for electric power expansion.

The land redistribution of 1967 was essentially a continuation of the Lopez Mateos land reforms initiated in 1962. Diaz Ordaz participated Oct. 29, 1967 in the distribution of $2\frac{1}{2}$ million acres of land to some 9,600 *ejidal* peasant families under the Mexican land reform program. The land, in Chihuahua State in northwestern Mexico, was made available by break-up of some of the country's last big estates (haciendas). The land was to be used mainly for cattle raising and was distributed to the peasants on the basis of continual usage but not outright ownership. The plots could be passed oh 'to heirs but not sold, leased or mortgaged. Diaz Ordaz, in ceremonies in the city of Chihuahua, passed out deeds to representatives of various peasant groups.

The World Bank May 21, 1969 announced approval of a $65 million loan to Mexico for a program aimed at increasing livestock and crop production. The loan was the first part of a new 5-year, $200 million Mexican agricultural credit program. $90 million was earmarked for the development of commercial cattle ranches in the southeastern section of the country and the remaining $110 million was slated for crop and livestock production and development of selected agro-industries.

The World Bank announced another $125 million loan to Mexico Feb. 25, 1970. The loan, to be combined with about $40 million from export financing institutions in major supplier countries, was to be applied to the foreign exchange costs of Mexico's nationwide electric power expansion program during 1970-1. Total capital investment in the 1970-1 program was projected at $491.4 million.

2 other developments during this period were the loss of Mexico's worldwide leadership in silver production and the increasing government control of radio and TV stations.

The Mexican government reported Feb. 22, 1969 that Canada had produced 45.6 million ounces of silver in 1968 and had displaced Mexico as the world's leading silver producer. Mexico, in 2d place, produced 41.6 million ounces.

The *BOLSA* (Bank of London and South America) *Review* reported in June, 1969 that Mexican radio and TV stations had been made subject to a 25% tax on income from services such as advertising. However, the tax, effective July 1, could be met by a subsidy of the same amount if the stations sold 49% of their equity to a special fund administered by the government. The measure had been inserted into 2 bills passed by the Mexican congress in 1968 and had caused speculation concerning the extent of government control over radio and television. The London news letter *Latin America* reported July 18 that TV stations would be allowed to give free time on the air to the government in lieu of the 25% tax payment.

ECHEVERRIA ADMINISTRATION: EARLY YEARS

Luis Echeverria Alvarez, an athletic, balding, 48-year-old lawyer and former university professor of *mestizo* descent, became Mexico's 26th elected president Dec. 1. 1970.

Time magazine described the new president as "a strong disciplinarian with a puritanical streak." Other publications considered him inscrutable and sphinx-like. The London newsletter *Latin America* made this comment on the eve of the new president's inauguration:

> The formidable task facing President-elect Echeverria Alvarez will be to restore ͺthe revolutionary mask which slipped badly under President Diaz Ordaz, but which is an essential factor in Mexico's stability. . . . [Echeverria] assumes office . . . in an atmosphere of greater political tension and uncertainty than has been felt in Mexico for a generation. . . . From the few indications which have emerged it seems clear that Echeverria will attempt to present himself in the 'populist' clothing assumed by Lazaro Cardenas and, to a lesser degree, Adolfo Lopez Mateos. . . . Echeverria is also laying great stress—even more, if possible, than recent presidents in their early days—on the agrarian problem, and he is making more emphatic use of Mexico's standard revolutionary phraseology. "I will continue the dynamic process of the revolution until the end," he declared recently—and much more in the same vein.

Echeverria soon gave indications that, despite his conservative record, he was moving toward the traditional center of the ruling PRI, (Institutional Revolutionary Party). He released almost all of the remaining prisoners from the 1968 Mexico City demonstrations, moved toward a new accommodation with the PRI's left wing and with leftists outside the party, and undertook a serious continution of the agrarian reforms of Lopez Mateos. And as predicted, Echeverria sought to brighten his image with some of the populist sheen still surviving from the Cardenas era. (Both Cardenas and Lopez Mateos had died not long before Echeverria's assumption of office, Lopez Mateos Sept. 22, 1969 and Cardenas Oct. 19, 1970.)

Echeverria had begun his his political career in the PRI in 1946, just after he had obtained the *licenciado* qualifying him to practice law. Joining the law faculty of the University of Mexico in 1947 as adjunct professor of political theory, he continued to perform various duties within the PRI "machine" and rose rapidly to the forefront of the party. After some experience in a variety of administrative posts, Echeverria became chief of the PRI's executive committee in Oct. 1957. In this capacity he directed the presidential campaign of Lopez Mateos.

In 1958, under Lopez Mateos, Echeverria became an undersecretary in the key interior ministry *(secretaria de gober-acion)*. Echeverria took over the interior portfolio himself in 1964 when Diaz Ordaz was inaugurated. As interior minister Echeverria was the 2d most powerful man in the country, as well as the heir-apparent.

During the Diaz Ordaz administration Echeverria was generally associated in the Mexican public's mind with Diaz' right-of-center position within the PRI. A staunch defender of "law and order," Echeverria had called out the troops who fired on the Tlatelolco demonstrators in Mexico City Oct. 2. 1968.

Echeverria Elected President

As the ruling Institutional Revolutionary Party's candidate, Luis Echeverria Alvarez won a decisive victory with 11,923,755 votes in the Mexican presidential election July 5, 1970. His opponent, Efrain Gonzalez Morfin of the PAN *(Partido de Accion Nacional)*, received 1,945,391 votes.

The number of citizens eligible to vote increased in 1970 to 21,700,000, from 13,598,594 in the 1964 general elections (3 million new voters had recently been added through a constitutional amendment lowering the voting age from 21 to 18), while the number of abstentions increased to 7,672,184 or 35% from 30.57% in 1964. In addition, the number of void ballots increased from 32,125 in 1964 to 158,670 in 1970.

The PRI won all 60 senatorial seats and 178 seats in the Chamber of Deputies. (About 13,794,500 voters failed to vote for legislative candidates in the 1970 election, and 447,829 of the ballots were void.)

In addition to PRI and PAN, 2 other parties—the left-wing PPS *(Partido Popular Socialista)* and the PARM *(Partido Autentico da la Revolucion Mexicana)*—presented candidates for the Chamber of Deputies and the Senate and for some state and local positions. The PPS polled 123,330 votes, and the PARM 75,921 votes.

Echeverria, interior minister since 1964, had conducted one of the most extensive campaigns ever undertaken by a Mexican presidential candidate. In a strenuous 7-month campaign he had visited every state in the nation, travelling more than 30,000 miles and speaking to voters in more than 850 municipalities. Stressing a continuation of the centrist policies of Pres. Diaz Ordaz, Echeverria pledged to upgrade the life of the peasant through national, state and local planning. He called for an increase in productivity through programs of credit and technical assistance, along with education and vocational training. He also stressed the importance of industrial decentralization through prohibition of the establishment of new industries in areas already highly industrialized and through incentives for investment in less industrialized regions. Bowing to Catholic opinion, he opposed any official action to reduce the nation's $3\frac{1}{2}\%$ annual population growth rate. (Mario Moya Palencia had been named interior minister Nov. 11, 1969, succeeding, for a brief period, Echeverria, who had resigned to run for president.)

There had been some question in 1969 whether the major opposition party, the pro-Catholic right-wing PAN, would oppose the PRI in the 1970 general elections. Following a disputed state election in Yucatan in November 1969, PAN had alleged government fraud and had threatened to withdraw its candidate from the presidential race. PAN chose in Jan. 25, 1970, however, to remain in the presidential campaign.

(Bitter feuding between the PRI and PAN continued into the Echeverria period. PAN charged in 1972 that the government had spent almost $50,000 of taxpayers' money to restore and improve buildings owned by the PRI. A PAN note said the expenditure had been confirmed by Public Works Min. Luis Enrique Bracamontes, who had told the Senate the money was spent on "social service works at the request of the PRI.")

Echeverria was inaugurated for his 6-year term Dec. 1, 1970. In his inauguration speech he pledged to continue agrarian reforms and industrial expansion and to implement a more independent foreign policy. Expressing faith in the eventual success of his proposed reforms, the new president pledged that the Mexican "revolution" would "continue in force until the very poorest have attained an adequate standard of living." Echeverria warned that "overconcentration of income and the marginal position of large groups threaten the harmonious continuity of our development." He stressed that "employment and productivity must be increased more rapidly, and to accomplish this it is indispensable to expand the domestic market and share income more equitably." He again opposed a government-sponsored birth control program to slow the rate of population growth. Asserting that "foreign investment should not displace Mexican capital," Echeverria said Mexico would accept "investors from different countries who, under the guidance of Mexicans, wish to establish new industries and contribute to the promotion of the continuous transfer of technology and the manufacture of articles for export to all markets, including their own."

5,000 guests attended the inauguration ceremonies, including delegates from more than 60 foreign nations. State Secy. William P. Rogers represented the U.S.

Echeverria's cabinet, named Nov. 30, included 3 members of ex-Pres. Diaz Ordaz' cabinet: Agriculture Min. Manuel Bernardo Aguirre, Finance Min. Hugo B. Margain and Atty. Gen. Julio Sanchez Vargas. Emilio O. Rabasa, Mexican ambassador to the U.S., was named foreign minister, while acting Interior Min. Mario Moya Palencia was named the permanent minister. Other cabinet minister included: *Defense* —Gen. Hermenegildo Cuenca Diaz: *Navy*—Adm. Luis Bravo Carrera; *National Treasures*—Horacio de la Pena; *Industry & Commerce*—Carlos Torres Blanco; *Communications & Trans-*

port—Eugenio Mendes; *Public Works*—Luis Enrique Braca-
montes; *Hydraulic Resources*—Leandro Rovirosa Wade; *Public
Education*—Victor Bravo Ahuja; *Health*—Jorge Jimenes Cantu;
Labor—Rafael Fernandez Ochoa. Alfonso Martinez Dominguez, head of the PRI and manager of Echieverria's campaign,
was appointed mayor of the federal district of Mexico.

Reyes Heads PRI

Jesus Reyes was named president of the ruling Institutional Revolutionary Party (PRI) Feb. 21, 1972 after the
resignation of Manuel Sanchez Vite. According to *Le Monde*
Feb. 22, Reyes' accession temporarily ended a serious crisis
within the party, whose "liberal" and "conservative" factions
were bitterly at odds. Sanchez Vite, who was close to friends
of ex-Pres. Gustavo Diaz Ordaz, allegedly had failed to put
into effect the "democratizing" policies of Pres. Luis Echeverria Alvarez. Reyes. was said to belong to the party's "liberal"
faction.

(The PRI won an overwhelming majority July 1, 1973
in elections for 194 federal deputies, 7 state governors and 87
mayors. The final count gave the PRI 69.55% of the total
vote and the major opposition group, the conservative PAN,
14.74%. The PRI took 189 of the 194 elective seats in the
Chamber of Deputies, to 4 for the PAN and one for the
Authentic Party of the Mexican Revolution. The PAN was
entitled to the maximum 25 additional Chamber seats awarded by proportional representation, since its share of the vote
exceeded 11½%. Initial reports said voter abstention was
low, but a report by the newsletter *Latin America* July 13 asserted it may have been as high as the 35% recorded in 1970.
The government had tried to stimulate interest by a series of
electoral reforms and a vigorous voter registration drive.
PAN leader Jose Angel Conchello charged July 4 that "electoral chieftainism has gained control of the entire republic,
and the elections were characterized by disorganization and
anarchy." PAN officials said they would contest results in 30
election districts.

(Earlier in 1973 Congress had approved a number of reforms in the national election laws. The reforms included awarding of free radio and TV time to all parties, reduction of the minimum age for election to the Senate from 35 to 30 and to the Chamber of Deputies from 30 to 21, and provisions for awarding more seats in the lower house to the small and virtually powerless opposition groups. Under the old proportional representation law, any political party gaining $2\frac{1}{2}\%$ of the national vote received a block of 5 Chamber seats. Every additional half per cent entitled the party to another seat, to a maximum of 20. Under the reformed law, the maximum was raised to 25 and the base required for the first 5 seats was reduced to $1\frac{1}{2}\%$. Opposition parties charged that the reform was only token, since it did not give them an opportunity to have a reasonable constituency in the Chamber. The ruling PRI controlled all 178 Chamber seats elected in individual districts, leaving for the opposition only the few seats awarded by proportional representation. The PRI also controlled the presidency and all 60 seats in the Senate.)

GROWING CIVIL UNREST

What many observers regard as the most remarkable social development during the early years of the Echeverria administration was the upsurge of dissent and unrest in many areas of Mexican life.

Left-wing students continued to provide the most obvious focus for discontent with the PRI-dominated government. But much criticism also came from the rest of the academic community and in fact from intellectuals in general. Peasants seized land, as they had during Lopez Mateos term. And, at the extreme left, least 2 hands of guerrillas mounted a campaign of violence throughout Mexico.

Echeverria Backs Monterrey Students

The federal government was said to have capitalized on a student controversy in the Nuevo Leon state university in

Monterrey in May 1971. The controversy led to the resigation of the governor of Nuevo Leon state, Eduardo Elizondo.

The dispute began when newly-elected rector Arnulfo Trevino Garza tried to take office in the university. A student strike was declared against the unpopular Trevino Garza, and strikers clashed with police on several occasions. In a surprise move, Echeverria sided with the students and forced Trevino Garza to resign. Subsequently Gov. Elizondo also resigned.

By siding with the students, Echeverria, it was said, did much to overcome resentment over his role in the 1968 disorders (as interior minister under Diaz Ordaz, Echeverria had been in charge of police and internal security).

According to some observers, however, there were other, veiled political reasons why Echeverria backed the students instead of the government, in Nuevo Leon. It was reported that the Echeverria regime intervened to avert a potentially dangerous student outbreak. Furthermore, the students were seen as opponents of the "establishment" families who controlled Monterrey's steel and brewery industries and who were known to be incensed at Echeverria's economic program. Trevino Garza was a member of Monterrey's powerful Garza family, and Gov. Elizondo, only recently connected with the right-wing PAN, had been an "establishment" lawyer. Education Min. Victor Brava Ahuja, who went to Monterrey to represent the Echeverria administration, persuaded the state congress to adopt a new university "organic law" embodying most of the student demands, and he secured the release of students and teachers who had been arrested. The administration thus appeased the students and weakened its right-wing opposition. (Sen. Luis Farias took over as governor of Nuevo Leon state.)

Corpus Christi Massacre Sparks Political Crisis

Grave disorders involving students and resulting in several violent deaths took place in Mexico City June 10, 1971 (Corpus Christi day). The Echeverria government, which was

committed to a more open and lenient policy, than its predecessor in dealing with left-wing students and the Mexican
left wing in general, opened an investigation of the Corpus
Christi disorders. According to many well-informed observers, the investigations caused a rift between the conservative
and the liberal wings of the PRI.

11 Students were killed and 160 wounded in the June 10
clashes between demonstrating students and armed groups of
right-wing extremists. The clashes began when a group of
8,000 leftist students began an anti-government march from
the National Polytechnic Institute in the north of the city to
the downtown area. They were soon confronted by a group
of 500 right-wing youths who attacked with automatic weapons while police stood by. There was disagreement over the
the identity of the armed right-wing group. Students said the
attackers were members of a group called the "Hawks" *(los
Halcones),* who were recruited by police. The government
first contended that a right-wing anti-government group
called MURO had engineered the attack to embarrass the
president, whom the group considered too liberal.

At a news conference June 11, a government spokesman
was unable to explain why police had been given orders not
to intervene. Government sources indicated June 13 that
there was evidence of collaboration between the Mexico City
police force and the Hawks, who were permitted to pass
through a police cordon to attack the students. Government
critics charged that policemen dressed as civilians fired into
the crowd. University authorities said the attackers had been
"organized by elements of considerable economic and material resources." (Marlise Simons, a Dutch correspondent who
was kidnaped for 5 hours by the rightists June 10, said she
had heard 2-way radios used and apparent references to
headquarters.) Several Mexican and foreign correspondents
were also reported attacked by rightist groups. The government spokeman stated that the attackers had "absolutely no
connection with the federal government," but many observers
disagreed.

Echeverria canceled a planned meeting with Nicaraguan

Pres. Anastasio Somoza June 11 and promised a thorough investigation of the clash. It was reported that he had planned to meet with the student demonstrators at the Zocalo to express agreement with their complaints and to enlist their backing in his struggle against the government's reactionary elements.

There was speculation that the attack was a plot by conservative elements of the party to weaken the position of Echeverria. It was reported they had the support of Mexico City Mayor Alfonso Martinez Dominguez, who was responsible for the maintenance of order in the capital. Martinez Dominguez and Police Chief Rogelio Flores Curiel resigned June 15. The resignations were submitted "in order to facilitate the official investigations" of the disorders authorized by Echeverria to seek out and arrest those responsible for the attacks.

Observers saw the resignations as part of an intense ideological power struggle within the PRI. Martinez Dominguez, considered the head of the party's conservative wing, had been chairman of the PRI under the Diaz Ordaz government. Students and journalists had charged that the Mexico City government under Martinez Dominguez had supported and helped to organize the "Hawks," whom many considered responsible for the attacks.

Most leading officials at city hall turned in their resignations to the new mayor, Octavio Senties, appointed June 17 by Echeverria. Senties was president of the Chamber of Deputies and leader of the PRI's peasant sector.

Enrique Herrera, undersecretary of communications and transport and president of the National Radio Commission, also resigned June 12. Herrera too was considered a member of the PRI's right wing.

About 300,000 workers, peasants and members of the middle class, mobilized by the Mexican Workers' Confederation, demonstrated in Zocalo square in front of the presidential palace June 15 in support of Echeverria. Echeverria told the gathering that not only "clandestine politics, but also provocation and repressive methods, conspire against the people and the revolution." He pledged to continue "the effort to liquidate exploitation and injustice."

(In a related development, the Mexican Communist Party June 21 issued a manifesto calling for the "overthrow of the oligarchy." The manifesto was intended as a rallying point for continued opposition to the Echeverria administration.)

After 42 days of investigation, Atty. Gen. Julio Sanchez Vargas said July 23 that those responsible for the killings could not be identified, although the Hawks had attacked the students. Sanchez said there was no proof that the Hawks were connected with the Mexico City government as some observers believed. Sanchez reported that city buses had been used to transport members of the Hawks to the student demonstrations. He said his office had found evidence that police on the scene had stood by passively while students were being killed because they were under instructions not to stop the student demonstration and had therefore not intervened

Hiram Escudero, PAN *(Partido de Accion Nacional)* legislative deputy, had accused the Mexico City government June 26 of being "directly responsible" for the incidents. Escudero said he personally had observed the killings and had presented proof of his charge to the attorney general's office. The opposition PAN demanded an "open door" meeting with Sanchez so that the "real" results of the official investigations could be revealed.

Sanchez Vargas resigned as attorney general Aug. 19 after admitting that his investigation into the student deaths had failed to turn up any suspects. He was replaced by Pedro Oleja Pallada, a senior official in the president's office.

(About 500 students defied a police ban and held a peaceful demonstration June 10, 1972 to mark the first anniversary of the "Corpus Christi massacre.")

Conciliation of Student Left

Pres. Echeverria continued to seek reconciliation with student leftists and other dissenters in the following months. The conciliatory move brought on renewed charges from the

PRI's right wing that he had moved to the left and "sold out" the party's law-and-order-oriented hard-liners.

A group of prominent leftist intellectuals and labor leaders in Sept. 1971 announced the formation of a new political organization to challenge the one-party system of the PRI (Institutional Revolutionary Party) which had ruled Mexico since 1929. Among the group's members were writers Octavio Paz and Carlos Fuentes, mining leader Manuel Santos and student leaders Heberto Castillo and Luis Cabeza de Vaca, who had both completed prison terms stemming from their role in the 1968 student movement. The principal aims of the new movement, aside from providing an alternative to the PRI, included further nationalization of banks and basic industries, strict control of foreign investment, an end to Mexican dependence on the U.S. through the opening of new export markets, union democracy, thorough agrarian reform and an equitable educational system.

At a press conference, Fuentes said the group would not adopt a formal name or announce a formal platform because the movement's purpose was not to impose another structure from above but to form an organization from below that reflected the political reality of Mexico. The group's leaders declared that "there is a restlessness in the country and a growing demand by Mexicans for a transformation of the present system." Fuentes admitted that, while a new party would have no chance of gaining power within the present political system, the political climate had changed somewhat since Echeverria had assumed power in 1970.

The *Washington Post* reported Sept. 23 that one of the group's principal concerns was to unite the forces of the left and to avoid the factionalization of the radical movement. The group reportedly disavowed the use of violence and guerrilla activities.

Echeverria met the following year in Veracruz state with leaders of the 1968 student protest movement. This was a move interpreted as sealing a government reconciliation with the moderate left.

The president was still championing a reformist approach

to Mexico's political and social problems. In his 2d annual state-of-the-nation address to Congress Sept. 1, 1972, Echeverria admitted corruption and incompetence in the government, greed and selfishness in the private sector and a need for changes in Mexico's institutions. He promised reforms in all 3 areas.

A communique from the National Action Party (PAN), Mexico's major opposition party, charged Aug. 7, 1972 that the government was directly responsible for the "constant violence and terror." Echeverria replied that the PAN was a "conservative force" which neither had nor would gain political power. The communique, signed by PAN leader Angel Conchello Davila, alleged that "an undeclared war exists between communal farmers and small landowners in the fields of Sinaloa and many other parts of the country," for which the government was responsible. Conchello charged that Mexico's universities were "crumbling." The National University was "practically under siege, surrounded by military bayonets," while universities in Puebla, Monterrey, Sinaloa and Veracruz were "focal points for violence directed in many cases by persons paid by local governments or influential politicians," he said. In the labor unions, Conchello charged, "more blood is spilled each day because the government and its party imposes and maintains leaders that have nothing to do with the workers' movement."

Student Unrest & Violence Continue

2 persons were killed and several wounded in Mexico City June 13, 1972 when a gun battle broke out between left-wing and right-wing groups at the Autonomous National University of Mexico (UNAM). The shootout reportedly followed several months of growing tension between opposing student factions struggling for control of the campus. According to the *Washington Post* June 14, the incident occurred after a group of students from the engineering faculty kidnaped several members of a rightist armed gang allegedly paid to keep organized opposition to the government at a minimum. The

rightists were reportedly being "tried" before a student assembly when another group of right-wingers invaded the auditorium to rescue them. 2 rightists were killed in the shootout that ensued. Conflicting reports, however, were filed by the *Miami Herald* June 15 and the newsletter *Latin America* June 16. According to the *Herald,* 2 students were shot to death by rightists as they painted political slogans around the university. According to *Latin America,* the students were killed as they demonstrated in supports of peasants.

Strict security measures were imposed in 5 cities July 25 following student disturbances involving bombings, street battles and mass arrests. There was no direct connection among incidents in the different cities, according to most reports. In Culiacan, capital of the western state of Sinaloa, students burned down the offices of the ruling Institutional Revolutionary Party in protest against the murder of 2 peasants who had pressed land claims. (A report Aug. 11 said 2 students were killed, many wounded and more than 200 arrested in disturbances following attempts by police and a right-wing paramilitary group to reinstate the rector of Culiacan's university, who had been expelled in April.) In Mexico City, students from the National University seized buses and held them as security for compensation that they demanded from the city's bus company on behalf of the family of a worker run over by a bus. Students reported fighting off armed police. In Puebla, near the capital, students demonstrated with teachers, peasants and workers in protest against the murder, apparently by right-wing terrorists, of Joel Arriaga Navarro, a left-wing architect and headmaster of the local university's preparatory school. Pres. Echeverria ordered a special investigation of the assassination. (The director of Puebla University's social services, Enrique Cabrera, was shot to death by unidentified men Dec. 21.)

Student riots were also reported in the northeastern city of Monterrey and the southeastern city of Oaxaca.

Public transportation in Culiacan, capital of the northwestern state of Sinaloa, was paralyzed beginning Oct. 6, 1972, by the action of students demanding compensation to the family of a worker run over by a bus at the beginning of the

month. More than 100 students had been arrested Oct. 4
following gun battles with police and the burning of several
buses. A policeman was wounded Oct. 14 in a shootout that
ensued when students tried to burn more buses in Culiacan.
(2 students had been killed and others wounded Apr. 7 as
police fired into a crowd of student demonstrators outside
the state congress building in Culiacan. The students, protesting a proposed university law and demanding the resignation of the Sinaloa University rector, reportedly had stoned
the congress building for 2 hours.)

The rector of the National University (UNAM) in Mexico
City, Pablo Gonzalez, resigned Nov. 18, 1972 after failing to
curb continuing student unrest and to find a solution to a
strike by the university's non-academic employes. The strike,
begun in October for recognition of the employes' union,
was joined early in December by workers at other Mexican
universities, and UNAM classes were suspended by a student
boycott in sympathy with the workers. Gonzalez authority
reportedly had been undercut by student occupation of the
university rectory 3 months previously. The leader of the
occupation, Miguel Castro Bustos, had been arrested. In
addition to ordinary criminial charges, he had been accused
of secretly working for right-wing terrorist groups.

Gonzalez' resignation followed the exposure by the
government of the "Pancho Villa" group, a band of right-
wing thugs trained by police officers in violent tactics to be
used against "progressive" students. The university's director
of information and public relations and the dean of the law
faculty were among officials linked to the group. Luis Gomez,
a former union official said to be the main obstacle to Pres.
Echeverria's reform plans for the PRI, was called the group's
originator. (Right-wing gangs of thugs known as "porras"
reappeared in Mexico City in Apr. 1973, attacking and in-
juring the director of the National Polytechnic Institute and
beating up a number of high school students and teachers.)

Guillermo Soberon, a U.S.-educated scientist, was chosen
rector of UNAM Jan. 4, 1973 to replace Gonzalez. Soberon's
inaugural, was marked by the occupation of his offices by

students, teachers and workers.

Classes at UNAM resumed Jan. 16, 1973 following the settlement of the strike. The strike ended when the university granted employes a 30% wage increase, a 5-day workweek and other benefits. The university did not, however, grant the employes' union a closed shop, leaving many students, lecturers and workers at odds over whether the employes' strike should continue.

In Puebla, 2 policemen posing as university students were kidnapped by students, who tortured and fatally shot one of them and wounded the other, the newsletter *Latin America* reported Feb. 9, 1973. The Puebla University rector blamed police and the Puebla state governor for infiltrating the university with secret agents, and held them responsible for the assassination of 2 university lecturers in 1972. A Puebla student had been reported killed Feb. 2 in clashes between students and police or right-wing strong-arm groups. A student was killed in similar clashes in Villa Hermosa, and another student was killed in Monterrey, according to the same report. 3 other Monterrey students had been wounded in clashes with police reported Jan. 19. In Guadalajara, the murder of 4 local student leaders by other youths was reported Feb. 17.

Students demanding the creation of a regional university in Torreon (in the state of Coachuila) seized Torreon's public transportation system Mar. 30, 1973 and blocked main roads out of the city. Their demand followed the refusal of a professor from the Torreon campus of the University of Coahuila to accept the university's rectorship in view of objections by students on the main campus in Saltillo, 170 miles east. Torreon authorities ultimately agreed to establish the new university. They said local state university facilities would become part of the new institution, to be called the Autonomous University of La Laguna.

4 students were killed and about 20 persons wounded May 1, 1973 in a shootout between police and students at the Autonomous University of Puebla. Students and authorities blamed each other for the incident. The violence began when police tried to stop about 300 students from joining a Labor Day

march in downtown Puebla. The students reportedly fought
with officers in the streets near the university and then seized a
university building, taking 3 police hostages with them. A 5-
hour shootout ensued in which 4 students were fatally wounded.
Students later released the police hostages, in exchange for 6
youths arrested by police, but continued to occupy the building.

Puebla students hijacked 14 city buses May 2 and used
them to blockade all streets leading to the university. Police
sealed off the area, but did not move against the students.
Another student was killed the next day after attending a
massive funeral service for the May 1 victims; police claimed
he was run over by a bus, but doctors said he had been struck
repeatedly with "a pipe or other blunt object."

Puebla state Gov. Gonzalo Bautista O'Farrell was sharply
criticized after the May 1 incident. Students accused him of
direct responsibility for the killings. The university rector,
Sergio Flores, charged May 2 that authorities had "provoked"
the incident by posting police sharpshooters near the main
university building. There were numerous calls for the governor's resignation. Bautista charged May 3 that students
sought his resignation "in order to continue dedicating themselves to vandalism and pillage. They don't want me because
I haven't allowed them to go on murdering, robbing and
kidnaping." He alleged that student violence in Puebla was
instigated by the Mexican Communist party, but he said he
was personally anti-Communist.

Bautista's resignation finally was announced May 10.
Meanwhile, the government in Mexico City had banned a
student march scheduled for May 9, in protest against the
Puebla killings. The traffic police chief, Daniel Gutierrez
Santos, said the demonstration had been organized by "students and other groups, especially the Communist party, which
are trying to alter the public order."

Government Harasses Foreign Critics

Despite the indications of a rapprochement between
Echeverria and the student left, considerable differences

remained between the government and left-tending intellectuals. There were instances of alleged government harassment
of intellectuals regarded as too unfavorable to the government
and foreigners were occasionally involved. Among instances
of action against presumed foreign critics in Mexico:

• Mrs. Rosario Valenzuela de Asturias, daughter-in-law of
Guatemalan Nobel Prize-winning writer Miguel Angel Asturias, was detained by Mexican secret police for 4 days Aug.
9-12, 1971. A statement issued by the Interior Ministry on her
release Aug. 12 said that Mrs. Valenzuela de Asturias had
been interrogated about alleged activities in violation of her
status as a political exile. She had been charged by the Mexican
government with engaging in subversive activities directed
against Guatemala. She was permitted to remain in Mexico
after she promised "not to continue such activities."

• Kenneth F. Johnson, a U.S. political science professor
who had written a book criticizing Mexican politics, was
deported Aug. 24, 1972 and later accused of authoring "false-
hoods and fantasies" about Mexico. Johnson, who taught
at the University of Missouri (St. Louis), had been in the
country to interview political dissidents for a revision of his
book *Mexican Democracy: A Critical Review.* He said he and
his family were arrested Aug. 21 and held until Aug. 23, when
he signed a statement admitting technical guilt on a diplomatic charge of intervening in Mexico's internal affairs.

• The government's chief public relations official, Fausto
Zapata, rebuked foreign correspondents in Mexico City for
allegedly reporting unfairly and unsympathetically on the
current administration, the *Miami Herald* reported Oct. 8,
1972. According to the *Herald,* Zapata reprimanded a *N.Y.
Times* correspondent for reporting a typhoid epidemic in
central Mexico in June; the epidemic was later confirmed by
officials. Zapata also reprimanded a British correspondent
for suggesting in an article that Pres. Echeverria had not carried out promised social reforms, the *Herald* reported. According to some observers, Zapata believed that in return for
favors from his office, foreign correspondents should report
on the government as favorably as did the Mexican press.

Payoffs to Mexican journalists, they contended, resulted in articles promoting government policies and extolling the president and top officials. (Many foreign correspondents in Mexico claimed that low salaries for reporters enabled the government systematically to bribe newsmen aud keep embarrassing news material out of the major newspapers.)

Sporadic Violence

There was other evidence of social unrest. Numerous violent incidents were reported. Among incidents reported in 1971:

● Melchor Ortega. 77, president in 1931-3 of the ruling PRI (then the PRN, *Partido Revolucionario Nacional*), was shot and killed along with his chauffeur in an ambush north of Acapulco (reported Mar. 10).

● Authorities reported that a shootout between Mexican troops and a group of unidentified men in the northwestern state of Sinaloa Apr. 8 had left at least 10 persons dead. Reports first said the troops had been attacked by bandits and marijuana growers when they entered a small village in Sinaloa, but according to other versions of the incident, the soldiers had fired first, without reason. *Le Monde* of Paris reported April 13 that the soldiers involved had been arrested.

● 2 peasants were killed and 5 injured May 3 in a battle between 2,000 peasants attempting to seize farmland and employes of the owners of the land near Ciudad Juarez on the Rio Grande. The peasants took the 2 owners of the property as hostages, and the land was reportedly offered after their release.

Church Liberals' Attack Conservatives

The increasing tensions in Mexican society appeared to be reflected in the internal politics of the Roman Catholic Church. Catholic liberals and conservatives clashed over the activities of the liberal clergy of Cuernavaca (a town near Mexico City). The bishop of Cuernavaca, Msgr. Sergio

Mendez Arceo, had been a supporter of CIDOC (Center for Intercultural Documentation), which had occasioned a 1969 controversy.

Mendez Arceo and the rector of the National Autonomous University, Pablo Gonzalez Casanova, had publicly opposed the sentences given to demonstrators in the 1968 student riots and called for a presidential amnesty.

The *N.Y. Times* Nov. 29, 1970 quoted Gonzalez Casanova as saying that the sentences had "sown doubts" in the university community concerning the viability of the "state of law" in Mexico. He added: "This sentiment of insecurity does not contribute in any beneficial way to the healthy development of the nation." (The university's 70,000 students struck Nov. 24 in support of an amnesty.) Mendez Arceo supported Gonzalez Casanova's appeal and claimed that an amnesty was necessary for political, democratic and humanitarian reasons.

A new intra-church controversy involved the publication in Sept. 1971 of a report backed by Mendez Arceo, in which Mexico's traditionally conservative Roman Catholic Church had criticized its own lack of action in opposing the oppression of the masses and in attacking social injustice in Mexico. The document had been prepared by an Episcopal Commission for Social Action for a scheduled World Synod of Bishops in Rome. The report, entitled "Justice in Mexico" and covering several aspects of national life, including the U.S. influence on Mexico, said that "in the silent but real oppression of classes and sectors in Mexico, the church seems to have played a role of spectator, if not of accomplice." The document discussed: the "marked affinity of the church towards economic power groups" which prevented it "from fulfilling its prophetic vocation"; a peasant class which suffered from "political and economic domination"; the social, economic and religious discrimination suffered by Indians; and the U.S.' hegemony over Mexico, which converted the latter into a "complement of [the U.S.'] . . . system as a peripheral and dominated country."

Mexico's trade union leaders and conservative Catholics

and politicians was reported Nov. 15, 1971 to have launched
an attack against reformist members of the Roman Catholic
clergy who criticized the country's social, economic and
political situation in the report. The progressive priests, led
by Mendez Arceo, were accused of violating the Mexican
constitution, which prohibited the church from involvement
in political matters.

Bishop Manuel Talamas y Camanadari and the priests
of his diocese in Feb. 1972 issued a statement in Ciudad
Juarez attributing a recent outbreak of kidnapings and robberies to "a desperate struggle for freedom and justice." The
priests said incidents of violence since the student disorders
of 1968 were not "isolated acts of common crime" but "links
in an ever-expanding chain," and often "the dramatic out-
cries of men who, having been systematically barred from
legal and democratic paths, have turned to violence as a
means of dealing with an even greater violence." The gap between rich and poor, the priests continued, was increasing
daily, and people "are oppressed by an unjust system that
denies them adequate participation at any level, economic,
political or cultural." Pres. Echeverria said Feb. 21 that political statements by priests, who were constitutionally barred
from paricipating in politics, were "within the wide range of
liberties in Mexico."

Corruption Attacked

National Patrimony Min. Horacio Flores de la Pena
admitted Feb. 16, 1972 that corruption was a great national
problem, and promised a campaign to eliminate it from
Mexican life. Flores called corruption "a true collective chain
of poison" causing "inefficiency of the country in solving its
ancestral problems." Atty. Gen. Pedro Ojeda Paullada later
invited citizens to file complaints with his office against cor-
rupt government officials or employes. The opposition National Action Party charged, however, that action based on
complaints was insufficient, and that an investigation of government corruption should be initiated. A spokesman for

the party said complaints were unnecessary when "the growing wealth of many officials is so ostentatious that it cannot
be explained by the salary they earn."

Ex-President Emilio Portes Gil broke a long political
silence Apr. 11, 1973 to criticize government corruption and
call for strict application of the law against "those who de-
fraud the people [and] oppress the peasants." "The immo-
rality we have reached has no parallel in our national history,"
Portes Gil said in a speech to some 2,000 peasants in Morelos,
62 miles from Mexico City, commemorating the 54th anniversary of the assassination of revolutionary leader Emiliano
Zapata. "The flag of the Mexican revolution is used for illegal
enrichment, while the entire country remains poor and ex-
ploited," Portes Gil asserted. The ex-president specifically attacked officials of state agrarian banks, who allegedly "robbed
and defrauded the impoverished peasants of the republic." He
said numerous cases of corruption, including a recent $1.6 mil-
lion fraud in the Yucatan Agrarian Bank had been denounced
to authorities, but officials had not pressed any investigations.

Another former president, Miguel Aleman Valdes, had
angrily denied reports that in 1948 he had planned with his
foreign minister, Jaime Torres Bodet, to allow U.S. oil companies to return to Mexico and compete freely with the state
concern Pemex, set up with an oil monopoly when the industry was nationalized 10 years earlier. The reports, cited
Feb. 2 with Aleman's denial, had arisen from publication in
the U.S. of State Department papers for the period. Econ-
omist Jesus Silva Herzog, said to be largely responsible for
drafting the nationalization documents, said Aleman had
signed exploration contracts with U.S. companies which
had cost Mexico $24 million to rescind 20 years later. These
contracts allegedly were a substitute for Aleman's original
plan, which was stopped by nationalist opposition in Mexico.
The Mexico City newspaper *Excelsior* had published other
documents purporting to show that another ex-president, the
late Manuel Avila Camacho, in office before Aleman, was
also implicated in plans to allow U.S. oil companies to return
to Mexico.

Guerrilla Activity; Soviet Aides Expelled

The Echeverria administration was plagued in 1971-3 by an upsurge of guerrilla activity. The guerrilla movement, similar to other such movements in Latin America, West Germany and the Middle East, appeared to be composed largely of students and intellectuals. The movement had 2 wings: an urban wing, known as the MAR *(Movimiento de Accion Revolucionario)*, and a rural wing, located in the mountainous southwestern state of Guerrero and apparently headed by ex-schoolteacher Genaro Vasquez Roja. Both used the same tactic of burglarizing civil commercial concerns and military arms convoys and magazines.

The first major confrontation between the government and the guerrillas occurred in Mexico City. The government claimed that the USSR and North Korea were responsible for the training of captured guerrillas.

The government announced Mar. 15, 1971, the arrest of the 19 Mexican revolutionaries whose leaders had allegedly studied in the Soviet Union in 1963 and had gone to North Korea in 1968-9 to study terrorism and guerrilla warfare.

The Mexican government Mar. 18, 1971 declared 5 members of the Soviet embassy in Mexico *persona non grata* and ordered them to leave the country "as soon as possible." The diplomats were Charge d'Affairs Dimitri Diakonov; First Secy. Boris Kolmiakov; 2d Secy. Boris Voskovoinikov; 2d Secy. Oleg Netchiporenko; and Alexandre Bolchakov, whose title was not given. All but Diakonov left the country Mar. 21; Diakonov remained behind to brief the Soviet ambassador to Mexico, Igor Kolosovsky, who had returned to Mexico City Mar. 20 from the Soviet Union where he had been on leave. Diakonov left Mexico for Havana Mar. 22.

The Mexican expulsion order gave no reasons for the action, but press reports connected it with the arrests announced Mar. 15 of the 19 Mexican revolutionaries. Mexican Atty. Gen. Julio Sanchez Vargas accused the Soviet Union of arranging and aiding the students' activities. The arrested revolutionaries said in a news conference Mar. 16 that they were members of the Revolutionary Action Movement (MAR).

Following the arrests, the Mexican ambassador to the Soviet Union, Carlos Zapate Vela, was recalled from Moscow Mar. 17 for consultations and what was called "a temporary diplomatic withdrawal."

In reaction to the expulsion of its diplomats, the Soviet embassy in Mexico City charged Mar. 18 that the action "serves only the interests of the enemies of the development of Mexican-Soviet relations." It added: "We do not understand, we do not know and we cannot explain the [Mexican] government's decision. . . ." (North Korean diplomats were also expelled. The *Miami Herald* reported Feb. 18, 1972 that police had arrested 4 MAR members who allegedly admitted receiving guerrilla training in North Korea.)

Mexico City Mayor Octavio Senties said in a TV statement July 22 that terrorists "with ties to the outside" had begun a campaign of assaults against banks, businesses and bus terminals in the city. He charged that an incipient urban guerrilla movement, the MAR, had intended "to destroy society" and was responsible for the recent assaults. Senties said the terrorist thefts "have all been executed in the same manner," by youths armed with machine guns or heavy rifles, using disguises and stolen cars.

The government announced July 21, 1971 the capture of 6 men and a woman accused of robberies to finance terrorist activities in Leon. Those arrested had in their possession rifles pistols, grenades and a large quantity of ammunition. The group was alleged to be part of an MAR guerrilla group centered in the state of Guerrero.

In a similar incident, government sources reported Sept. 12 that 5 men and one woman who robbed a bank in Leon Sept. 9 were members of the MAR.

The government ordered banks to tighten security measures Jan 18, 1972 in the wake of robberies and shootouts in the northern cities of Chihuahua, Monterrey and Aguascalientes. According to *La Prensa* of Buenos Aires Jan. 19, urban guerrillas took 300,000 pesos ($24,000) from a Monterrey bank Jan. 14, and 500,000 pesos ($40,000) from 3 Chihuahua banks the following day. The *Miami Herald* reported Jan. 18 that 3 persons were killed in a shootout between robbers and police outside one of the Chihuahua banks, and *La Prensa* said that 2 persons were killed in a similar battle in Aguascalientes Jan. 16. (About 200 students ran through the streets of Monterrey Jan. 19, throwing rocks and painting leftist slogans on the fronts of stores. They allegedly demanded a burial with honors for a student killed Jan. 17 by police searching for bank robbers.)

In his first state of the nation address since taking office Dec. 1, 1970, Pres. Echeverria Sept. 1, 1971 had warned extreme leftists against taking the law into their own hands and argued that violence would lead only to anarchy. Echeverria also said that recent robberies in Mexico had been the work of subversive groups "connected with underground movements from abroad." The president said Mexico's economic growth continued to be impressive, but he warned of the persistent unequal distribution of wealth and of problems dealing with peasants, education and urban growth.

Guerrillas based in the mountains of Guerrero state were officially charged with the kidnaping of a wealthy banker and distributing the ransom among the poor peasants of the area, according to a Sept. 11 report. The commander of the Guerrero guerrilla group, Genaro Vasquez Rojas, was also held reponsible for the death of another kidnap victim and for 15 other robberies and kidnapings.

2 major political kidnapings took place in Mexico in September and November 1971. (Kidnapings of well-known persons for political purposes had previously occurred in other countries.)

Police reported that Julio Hirschfeld Almanda, 54, industrialist and director of the nation's airport system, had been kidnaped Sept. 27, 1971 by 3 armed men and a woman. They were said to be members of the MAR. Hirschfeld was released unharmed Sept. 29 after payment of $91,000 in ransom. (Police Sept. 28 imposed special security precautions for Mexican officials and foreign diplomats as a result of the kidnaping. All senior government officials and diplomats were put under special police protection. Heavily armed guards had earlier been stationed outside all banks and telegraph offices after a wave of assaults.) According to the *Washington Post* Nov. 29, the Hirschfeld abduction later appeared to have been carried out by a right-wing group to provoke government repression of the left. The group, called FUZ *(Frente Urbano Zapatista,* Zapatist Urban Front, an allusion to the Mexican revolutionary Emiliano Zapata), claimed credit for the kidnaping and was reported Nov. 27, to have announced that it had distributed $24,000 of the $240,000 ransom to the poor of Mexico City. Mexico City police announced Jan. 31 that they had arrested 7 FUZ members in connection with the Hirschfeld kidnaping.

In another kidnaping incident, the Mexican government agreed Nov. 28, 1971 to exchange a group of political prisoners for the life of a kidnap victim, Dr. Jaime Castrejon Diez, rector of the State University of Guerrero, who was kidnaped on his way to work Nov. 19. Castrejon Diez, millionaire owner of the Coca-Cola bottling concession in Guerrero, was released Dec. 1, 2 days after his family paid a $200,000 ransom and 9 political prisoners (8 men and one woman) were flown to Cuba, where they were accepted by the Castro government for "humanitarian reasons." The kidnaping was believed to be the work of the guerrilla movement commanded by Genaro Vasquez Rojas. 5 of the prisoners exchanged were said to be close associates of Vasquez Rojas and the woman was said to be his sister-in-law. The kindnapers had also demanded that a 2d group of 15 political prisoners, currently held incommunicado, be brought to trial. The government made no public response to this demand.

Vasquez Rojas was killed Feb. 2, 1972, in the state of Michoacan, in what Mexican officials described as a car accident. Conflicting reports cited in U.S. newspapers Feb. 3 maintained, however, that Vasquez Rojas died in a shootout with agents of the Ciudad Hidalgo judicial police. Vasquez Rojas had been sought by police since 1968, when he escaped from prison after serving 2 years of a life sentence for agitation and killing a policeman. Vasquez Rojas had recently led the Southern Liberation Army (ELS), one of Mexico's most active guerrilla movements, which operated in the mountains of Guerrero. Members of the ELS had been hunted by the Mexican army since Nov. 1971, when they were accused of kidnaping the rector of the University of Guerrero. The group had been charged with robberies and other kidnapings, and with distributing ransom money among impoverished peasants. Vasquez Rojas' death was followed by the discovery of ELS camps, stores and information networks, and by the arrest of 8 members of the movement Feb. 8 in Chipalcingo.

(33 political prisoners jailed for 6 years on charges of storing arms and fomenting revolution were released Mar. 2, 1972. Among them was journalist Victor Rico Galan, accused of leading a guerrilla group.)

Armed men ambushed an army truck in the state of Guerrero June 25, 1972, killing 10 soldiers and escaping with a cargo of medicine and food supplies. 10 more soldiers were killed and 2 seriously wounded in Guerrero June 25 in an ambush by alleged members of the Zapatist Urban Front (FUZ). 17 persons were arrested in connection with the incident, and police were reported combing the mountains of the state in pursuit of guerrilla leader Lucio Cabanas.

A number of soldiers were killed Aug. 23, 1972 when guerrillas ambushed 2 army trucks in the mountains of Guerrero. The Defense Ministry said Aug. 24 that 7 soldiers had been killed, but the military commander in the area, Gen. Joaquin Solano, said Aug. 25 that 18 soldiers had died. Guerrilla leader Cabanas, in letters sent to 5 newspapers, reportedly took credit for the ambushes. 17 alleged guerrillas detained in Acapulco were charged with complicity in the ambushes.

During Mexico's Independence Day celebrations Sept. 16, 1972, there were at least 12 bomb explosions in 4 cities. They injured one person and caused considerable property damage. 7 of the blasts reportedly damaged U.S.-owned businessses.

4 members of the Armed Communist League, a small

guerrilla group, hijacked a Mexican airliner with 75 passengers in Monterrey Nov. 8, 1972. They flew the plane to Havana after obtaining arms, the release of 5 imprisoned comrades, a government promise to drop charges against 2 fugitive comrades and a ransom of about $330,000. Cuba returned the plane and passengers Nov. 9 but kept the 11 guerrillas and the ransom. Mexico asked for the extradition of 7 of the guerrillas Nov. 16, but Cuba refused Nov. 30 on the ground that their action was "political." The 5 prisoners released to the hijackers reportedly had been arrested in Monterrey Nov. 7 during a police search for guerrillas. Police action intensified in Monterrey and Mexico City Nov. 10. In reporting on the operation, the Mexican press admitted the existence of urban guerrillas for the first time.

Police were reported Mar. 23, 1973 to have announced the arrest of 10 guerrillas in Guerrero State and seizure of a large cache of arms. Guerrillas said, however, that an even larger consignment of arms had already been sent into the mountains.

3 policemen were reported Apr. 6, 1973 to have been shot to death in a clash with guerrillas commanded by Lucio Cabanas near the Pacific resort of Acapulco.

6 peasants in the village of Peloncillo (Guerrero State) were executed by soldiers Apr. 25 after being accused of sending food supplies to Cabanas' guerrilla group, the mayor of the village reported. The official said the victims' wives and relatives had been forced to dig graves for them. The executions reportedly followed the murder of a kidnaped local landowner by the Cabanas group after his family refused to pay $240,000 ransom. The army, which had launched a strong anti-guerrilla offensive in Guerrero, said it had arrested Cabanas' cousin, Manuel Garcia Cabanas, it was reported May 4. A female relative of Cabanas was said May 11 to have been detained and severely tortured, and 4 of her relatives reportedly disappeared.

U.S. Consul Kidnaped & Ransomed

The U.S. consul general in Guadalajara, Terrance G. Leonhardy, was kidnaped by left-wing guerrillas May 4, 1973 and freed unharmed May 7 after the Mexican government agreed to a number of demands, including freedom and safe conduct to Cuba for 30 alleged political prisoners. Payment of $80,000 ransom was also reported.

The freed prisoners, 26 men and four women, arrived in Havana on a Mexican airliner May 6. They asserted on reaching Cuba that they would return to Mexico to fight the government. Mexican authorities called them "common delinquents," but press sources said most of them belonged to urban guerrilla groups, which had carried out other kidnapings and bank robberies. The best known of those released was Jose Bracho Campos, an associate of the late guerrilla leader Genaro Vasquez Rojas.

Leonhardy was kidnaped by members of the People's Revolutionary Armed Forces, who demanded May 5 that the government: free the prisoners and transport them to Cuba; order the national press to publish a guerrilla communique; suspend the police and military search for Leonhardy; and allow the Cuban ambassador to go on TV to confirm the safe arrival in Havana of the prisoners.

Pres. Echeverria quickly agreed to meet the demands, saying his government prized human life highly. The U.S. reiterated its stance against yielding to extortion or blackmail for the release of officials abroad, and left the matter in Mexican hands.

The demands were met May 6, but Leonhardy was not released for another day, leading to speculation that the guerrillas had demanded other concessions from the government. The governor of Jalisco State, Alberto Orozco Romero, said May 8 that Leonhardy's wife had paid the guerrillas $80,000 ransom, which she had borrowed from a local bank. The U.S. had reportedly indorsed the loan, but the State Department denied this May 8. Jalisco State Gov. Alberto Orozco Romero said May 9 that Leonhardy would be responsible for paying back the borrowed $80,000 ransom money.

The guerrilla communique published in the press May 6 and broadcast over TV and radio, denounced Mexico's low health standards, its illiteracy and exorbitant credit rates, blaming the misery of impoverished workers and peasants on the concentration of wealth in the hands of a few, the outflow of Mexican capital abroad, and government repression of students, workers and peasants who tried to organize against authorities. The guerrillas denounced the government for trying to "convince the people that we are common delinquents, hired killers, cattle rustlers, enemies of the country. Today, for the first time and not voluntarily, the mass media are serving the proletarian cause."

Police claimed May 9 to have arrested 5 persons in connection with the Leonhardy kidnaping. "Dozens of others" had also been detained for interrogation in the case, *La Prensa* of Buenos Aires reported May 10. The area around Guadalajara had been sealed off. and federal police and soldiers had joined in the search for the kidnappers.

FOREIGN RELATIONS

Echeverria's Travels

Pres. Echeverria began a series of foreign trips in 1972 in a program to increase Mexican exports and widen foreign contacts.

Echeverria flew to Tokyo Mar. 9, 1972 for a 5-day visit and talks with Japanese Premier Eisaku Sato and leading Japanese bankers and industrialists. Echeverria returned to Mexico Mar. 14 after receiving promises of Japanese loans and increased imports of Mexican products. As a result of the visit, Japan was considering a joint venture to manufacture telephones in Mexico, the newsletter *Latin America* reported Mar. 31. Mexico's need was estimated at 2 million phones, and Japan reportedly was interested in penetrating the Latin American phone market.

Echeverria flew to Santiago Apr. 17, 1972 after stopping in Lima Apr. 16 to confer with Peruvian Pres. Juan Velasco Alvarado. Before returning to Mexico Apr. 21, Echeverria issued a joint communique with Chilean Pres. Salvador Allende calling for closer relations between Mexico and the

Andean Group, reaffirming the right of nations to control
their natural resources, and condemning economic or political pressures by any nation to prevent another from transform-
ing its own internal structures.

Echeverria addressed the 3d United Nations Conference
on Trade & Development (UNCTAD) in Santiago Apr. 20.
He warned that the new round of General Agreement on
Tariffs & Trade (GATT) talks planned by the U.S., European
countries and Japan could negate the advantages sought for
the poorer nations at the UNCTAD proceedings. He proposed that UNCTAD establish direct links with GATT to
guarantee participation in the talks by all developing nations,
whether or not they were members of the trade organization.
Echeverria urged the conferees to adopt a "charter of economic duties and rights of states," which would include the
demands of Chile's Socialist government for the renunciation
of economic pressure on other states and the express prohibition of interference by multinational corporations in the
internal affairs of the countries in which they operated.
Echeverria hailed Chile's nationalization of U.S. copper interests, recalling Mexico's expropriation in 1938 of foreign
oil companies.

Echeverria toured the U.S. June 14-21, 1972, conferring
with Pres. Richard M. Nixon in Washington June 15-16
and then visiting New York, Chicago, San Antonio and Los
Angeles. Mexico secured concessions from the U.S. on pol-
lution of the Colorado River, but the issue of trade was
unresolved. In a joint communique released June 17, the 2
countries pledged to study the problems of Mexican migrant
workers who entered the U.S. for seasonal employment, and
to continue efforts to halt the international narcotics traffic.
The U.S. also agreed to take steps to improve the quality of
water flowing from the Colorado River into Mexico.

Echeverria addressed a joint session of the U.S. Congress June 15, charging that the U.S. was ignoring problems
with its allies while trying to solve conflicts with its "enemies."
Referring to Nixon's recent attempts to reach accommodation with the Soviet Union and China, Echeverria said Mexico

and other "3d world" nations could not agree with "those who try to reduce world politics to dealings among powerful nations." Echeverria called it "impossible to understand why the U.S. doesn't use the same boldness and imagination that it applies to solving complex problems with its enemies to the solution of simple problems with its friends."

Echeverria flew June 17 to New York, where he sharply criticized U.S. economic behavior in Mexico, citing takeovers of Mexican corporations and other actions such as the sale of gasoline below cost on the U.S.-Mexican border. At a meeting with 2 dozen New York intellectuals in which he was criticized for the alleged lack of political freedom in Mexico, Echeverria argued that it was more important for his country to gain freedom to acquire U.S. technology while securing simultaneous freedom from U.S. domination.

Before returning to Mexico, Echeverria dedicated the Mexican Cultural Institute, a branch of the University of Mexico in San Antonio. The dedication, attended by about 4,000 persons, was picketed by a group demanding release of 200 alleged political prisoners held in Mexican jails.

Echeverria's World Tour

Echeverria visited 6 countries on 3 continents Mar. 29-Apr. 26, 1973 on what he called a "mission of peace" to promote Mexican political and economic interests and to defend the position of "3d world" countries against pressure from the great powers. Echeverria visited Canada, Britain, Belgium, France, the Soviet Union and China. The highlight of the tour was said to be agreement by France and China to sign the 2d protocol of the Treaty of Tlatelolco, under which nuclear powers pledged not to use or threaten to use nuclear arms in Latin America.

The tour reportedly was calculated to assert Mexico's independence from the U.S. by including visits to the 3 major world groupings outside it—the Soviet Union, China and the European Economic Community (EEC). (Echeverria met with U.S. Presidential adviser Henry Kissinger shortly before beginning his trip but did not release details of the talks.)

The tour, it was reported, was also intended to build support for Echeverria among Mexican leftists and to strengthen the president in his battle for reform against the right. Echeverria was the first Mexican chief executive to visit Moscow and Peking, and the first Latin American president to visit China since the Communist takeover there in 1949.

In Canada Mar. 29-Apr. 2, Echeverria conferred with Prime Min. Pierre Elliott Trudeau and other officials on ways to strengthen ties between their countries, particularly through increased trade and economic cooperation. He urged the Canadian Parliament Mar. 30 to work for coordination of Mexican and Canadian efforts to control foreign investments and curb the powers of multinational corporations. Echeverria urged in Toronto Mar. 31 that Canada and Mexico jointly oppose any attempts by the U.S. Senate to erect protectionist trade barriers. A joint communique issued by Echeverria and Trudeau Apr. 2 supported Mexican initiatives for a UN charter of economic rights and duties for all countries. Before departing for Europe, Echeverria said that Cuba should be readmitted to the Organization of American States.

Echeverria arrived in England Apr. 2 and was greeted officially by Queen Elizabeth the next day. He conferred Apr. 4 with Prime Min. Edward Heath, reportedly urging closer ties between the EEC and Latin American regional trade organizations, and asking British support for his proposed UN charter. Echeverria said Apr. 6 that Mexico supported other Latin American nations claiming 200-mile offshore territorial limits.

Echeverria toured Belgium Apr. 6-9. He met with Premier Edmond Leburton, other Belgian officials and EEC aides, asking for closer trade relations and gaining Belgian support for the proposed UN charter.

During his visit to France Apr. 9-12, Echeverria conferred with Pres. Georges Pompidou, who agreed with unspecified "reservations" to sign the Tlatelolco protocol. Observers noted, however, that the French cabinet had not yet approved the move. France also agreed Apr. 10 to grant Mexico an unspecified loan but stressed that the credit would be consistent with EEC investments in Latin America and would not give Mexico special privileges that might alienate other countries.

Echeverria met Apr. 11 with Argentine ex-Pres. Juan Peron, who flew to Paris to confer with him. Peron (whose protege Hector Campora later became president of Argentina May. 25) said he shared Echeverria's dissatisfaction with the structure of the OAS and supported his call for international control of multinational corporations.

(The Spanish government Apr. 14 issued a formal protest against assertions by Echeverria in Great Britain and France that Mexico would continue to deny recognition to the Franco government. Mexico recognized the Spanish Republican-government-in-exile, which had its seat in Mexico City.)

Echeverria visited the Soviet Union Apr. 12-19, talking with Communist Party General Secy. Leonid Brezhnev and other officials on ways to increase the dwindling trade between the 2 countries. He reportedly asked for Soviet adherence to the Tlatelolco protocol but did not obtain it.

Echeverria toured China Apr. 19-24, conferring with Premier Chou En-lai and other officials. The 2 countries Apr. 22 signed a one-year commercial treaty that granted mutual seaport facilities and gave Mexico most-favored-nation trade status with China. China also agreed to sign the Tlatelolco protocol.

Trade Options Expanded

The *Journal of Commerce* reported Sept. 28, 1971 that Mexico had decided to increase its trade in Europe and Asia, possibly including the Communist bloc countries, and reduce its trade with the U.S. The report said the decision was taken after Mexico became convinced of U.S. "discrimination" against Latin American countries in recent economic policies put into effect by Pres. Richard M. Nixon. Pres. Echeverria reportedly gave Finance Min. Hugo Margain instructions to diversify Mexican markets in both Europe and Asia. It was also decided that Mexico would attempt to head a Latin American bloc seeking a new trade policy as a result of U.S. economic protectionism.

In an effort to increase trade with other Western Hemisphere nations, Mexico took steps to improve economic relations with Canada and Cuba in 1971.

Mexico and Canada agreed to work toward a lessening of restrictions on commercial, cultural, and other relations. A communique, issued Oct. 22, 1971 after 2 days of talks in Ottawa between Mexican Foreign Min. Emilio Rabasa and Canadian External Affairs Min. Mitchell Sharp, also expressed a joint hope for the "earliest possible removal" of a 10% import surcharge imposed by the U.S. under a new, temporary economic control policy.

Mexico and Cuba were reported Dec. 2, 1971 to have signed an agreement establishing direct trade between the countries for the first time since 1959. Previously, trade between Cuba and Mexico had been conducted through Canada and payments for goods made through Canadian banks. Mexico and Cuba agreed July 7, 1971 to renew their bilateral air treaty, due to expire Aug. 11, for at least one more year. The current treaty had been renounced by Mexico in July 1970 after Cuba refused to extradite the hijacker of a Mexican airliner. Cuban Amb. Joaquin Hernandez Armas said that Cubana Airlines would continue its twice weekly flights between Havana and Mexico City. (A Mexican trade delegation visited Cuba in Mar. 1973 in an effort to sell more agricultural and industrial goods in exchange for Cuban nickel and rum. Under a signed agreement, Cuba contracted to buy $6.4 million worth of Mexican exports.)

The foreign ministers of Mexico and 12 other Caribbean countries met in Caracas, Venezuela for a 3-day informal conference and adopted Nov. 26 a resolution that laid the groundwork for a possible agreement on offshore fishing limits in preparation for the UN conference on territorial waters in 1973. The group also adopted a resolution calling on the U.S. to eliminate "as soon as possible the 10% surcharge on imports." Other issues discussed included transportation, communications, tourism and trade within the Caribbean. Attending the Nov. 24-26 meeting were representatives of Mexico, Venezuela, Colombia, Panama, Costa Rica, El Salvador, Guatemala, Nicaragua, Haiti, the Dominican Republic, Jamaica, Barbados and Trinidad & Tobago.

At another meeting to improve Caribbean commerce, Pres. Echeverria and Pres. Anastasio Somoza of Nicaragua signed an 8-point joint declaration, released Aug. 8, 1971, aimed at increasing trade between the 2 countries.

Mexico's Banco Nacional de Comercio Exterior was reported Sept. 8, 1972 to have concluded a banking agreement with Poland, Rumania and Yugoslavia in an effort to boost trade with Eastern Europe.

The U.S. opened a $450,000 trade center in Mexico City Feb. 14, 1972 in apparent response to growing Japanese and European economic activity in Latin America. U.S. Commerce Secy.-designate Peter G. Peterson said the U.S. sought to stimulate Mexican industrial exports by providing expertise and equipment, and to consolidate its own economic position in the area. The *Washington Post* commented Feb. 15 that Peterson's presence in Mexico City showed the importance given by the Nixon Administration to trade relations with Mexico, the U.S.' 5th largest trading partner. The U.S. bought 67% of Mexico's exports and provided 70% of its imports. Mexico had complained in recent months of U.S. protectionist tendencies, which had limited imports of Mexican manufactured goods and threatened the country's border industrialization program. Peterson, the *Post* reported, sought to reassure Mexico and other Latin American countries that the Nixon Administration was trying to liberalize trade, but that its hands were tied by Congress.

The Mexican government concluded several important international economic agreements in 1972: A $96.4 million IDB (Inter-American Development Bank) loan to helpd evelop Mexico's fishing industry was confirmed Sept. 15. The IDB was reported Oct. 4 to have approved a $35 million loan to help Mexico finance its National Plan of Irrigation Works for Rural Development, designed to improve the lot of poor rural communities in each of the nation's 6 geographic regions.

(The Foreign Trade Institute reported in Mar. 1973 that Mexican exports had risen by 22.9% in 1972. Mexico again had a large trade surplus with other Latin American Free Trade Association countries in 1972, with exports of $140.7 million and imports of $119.7 million, it was reported Mar. 9.)

U.S. Relations

Mexico and the U.S. in Apr. 1972 signed a treaty aimed at settling existing boundary disputes, and the 2 countries established mechanisms for resolving future territorial conflicts. The accord provided for restoration and maintenance of the Colorado River and the Rio Grande as continuous natural boundaries, and incorporated procedures to guard against future loss of territory by either country from shifts in river flow. It also established maritime boundaries between Mexico and the U.S. in the Pacific Ocean and the Gulf of Mexico.

A furor was touched off in the government and press by an Apr. 15, 1973 *N.Y. Times* report describing an apparently illegal system under which Mexicans seized illegally entering the U.S. were removed to the interior of Mexico against their will. The report disclosed how Mexican and U.S. border officials put thousands of illegal emigrants annually on privately owned Mexican buses and airplanes which took them to the Mexican interior at their own expense. The report also disclosed that if the aliens paid off the bus and airline operators they were released at the Mexico-U.S. border or near it. According to federal grand jury testimony in California and immigration authorities on both sides of the border, the aliens violated no Mexican law and thus should not have been transported hundreds of miles into Mexico before being released. Mexican government sources said Pres. Echeverria had ordered an investigation of the removal program and had discussed the issue with Pres. Nixon in Washington in June 1972.

U.S. State Secy. William P. Rogers visited Mexico and 7 countries in Latin America and the Caribbean during May 1973, conferring with government officials in an attempt to begin what he called "a new era of interest and cooperation" between the U.S. and other hemispheric nations. Rogers, in Mexico May 12-14 met May 12 with Foreign Min. Emilio Rabasa, and the next day with Pres. Echeverria. After the 2d meeting, Rogers said he had presented "a concrete and serious proposal" to end the long-standing dispute between the U.S. and Mexico over the high salinity of Colorado River water flowing into Mexico.

Preliminary details of the anti-salinity plan were reported by the *Wall St. Journal* June 4, 1973. According to the *Journal,* the U.S. had decided to build the world's largest desalination plant to improve the quality of Colorado River waters flowing into Mexico. Planning of the plant, to cost an estimated $60 million to $70 million, was indirectly confirmed to U.S. Congressmen by Interior Undersecy. Jack Horton, the *Journal* reported. The plan was said to have been approved by Mexican officials, and to enjoy wide support in the U.S. Congress as the best solution to Mexico's decades-old complaint that farming in the Mexicali Valley in Baja California was being damaged by salinity in the lower Colorado. As currently envisioned by the Interior Department's Office of Saline Water, the plant would remove about 90% of the salt from water in the channel draining the Wellton-Mohawk irrigation project of southern Arizona. It would be capable of treating 130 million to 140 million gallons of water daily.

Echeverria was reported June 29, 1973 to have reiterated his intention to extend Mexico's 12-mile offshore territorial limits to 200 miles. Seafood industry officials in the U.S. said the move would cost the industry $35 million to $40 million a year, since it would place most of the rich shrimp beds off Mexico's southern coast off limits to foreign boats.

Ties with China, Guyana & East Germany

Mexico and mainland China formally established diplomatic relations during 1972. Mexico's first ambassador to

China, Eugenio Anguiano Roch, arrived in Peking Aug. 6. The presentation of credentials by the first Chinese ambassador in Mexico City was reported Aug. 9. (The Mexican Communist party announced Aug. 11 that it had re-established ties with the Chinese Communist party following a visit to Peking by its leader, Arnoldo Martinez.) China and Mexico issued a joint communique in Peking Oct. 27 announcing a future increase in trade between the 2 countries.

Mexico agreed in Mar. 1973 to exchange ambassadors with Guyana, the last independent country in the Western Hemisphere with which it did not have diplomatic relations.

Mexico and East Germany established diplomatic relations June 5, 1973.

ECONOMIC DEVELOPMENTS

Despite continuing high GNP growth, unemployment and inflation became threatening problems in the early 1970s. The inflation of the peso was largely a consequence of inflationary pressure from the U.S. dollar. Mexico devalued the peso Feb. 12, 1973 to maintain parity with the devalued U.S. dollar. The move was followed by an increase in food prices, with some items rising 50% or more. According to news reports Mar. 23, 1973, food price patrols of policewomen had begun to operate in Mexico City to keep shopkeepers from raising prices excessively.

The Banco Nacional de Mexico, the country's 2d biggest bank, warned in Sept. 1970 that an "inflationary spiral" threatening the country could have drastic effects on its growth prospects. The Bank reported that the 5% price increase in 1970's first half had been caused largely by fear of U.S. price raises and partly by such domestic factors as a new labor law giving workers substantial concessions, new labor contracts and increased prices of steel and some raw materials.

Mexico's employment problems were also worsening, with an estimated 3½ million persons out of work and another 5 million marginally employed part of the year, it was reported Oct. 4, 1972. Half the nation's population earned only 10%

of the gross national product (GNP), and 10% of the population earned 50% of the GNP, the Finance and National Patrimony Ministries reported. The Mexican Workers Confederation, affiliated with the governing Revolutionary Institutional party, held a demonstration in Mexico City Feb. 25, 1973 as part of a campaign to establish a 5-day, 40-hour week. Most Mexican workers worked 6 days a week.

(According to government estimates of June 7, 1972, more than 350,000 Mexican children died annually from malnutrition and more than half of the Mexican population was undernourished.)

Inflation during the first 4 months of 1973 reached $8\frac{1}{2}$%, more than the rise planned for the entire year. Old economic problems were simultaneously emerging, including rising foreign indebtedness and a chronic trade deficit, currently about $1¼ billion a year. Government statistics reported May 25, 1973 showed that 45% to 50% of Mexico's families had incomes of less than $80 a month.

The government in early 1972 had instituted a wide-ranging series of changes in import-duty regulations to stimulate imports of machinery and equipment not produced in Mexico and spur industrial development. The measures included a 65% import-duty subsidy to companies using imported equipment not produced in Mexico.

In what was generally regarded as the culmination of a dispute over governmental economic policy, Finance Min. Hugo Margain, reported to be at odds with Pres. Echeverria, resigned for "health reasons" May 29, 1973 and was replaced by Jose Lopez Portillo, an administrator considered loyal to to the president. The development caused an outcry from private business, which charged that the government's "vague" policies had caused agricultural production to fall and inflation to accelerate. The Chamber of Commerce accused the government June 2 of "buying inflation" with its recent importation of $320 million worth of wheat, corn, powdered milk and other food items. There were reports June 9 of the hoarding of U.S. dollars, leading to fears of a devaluation of the peso. Lopez Portillo charged that the hoarding was the work of "coward, catastrophists and satanists." Margain was reported to have disagreed strongly with the government's policy of intervening in the private sector by purchasing shares in private firms. Lopez Portillo, a former aide to ex-Pres. Gustavo Diaz Ordaz, was replaced as director of the National Electricity Commission by Arsenio Farel, president of the Sugar Chamber and a former law partner of Echeverria's brother.)

'Mexicanization' Continues

Echeverria gave several indications that he would continue the long-standing government policy of "Mexicanizing" foreign firms in Mexico.

The government announced Aug. 27, 1971 that Mexico's small copper industry would be nationalized. The Anaconda Co. said the same day that it would sell 51% of the stock in its Mexican mining operation to the Mexican government and to private investors in the country. Mexican National Properties Minister Horacio Flores de la Pena said the government would pay Anaconda $40 million over a 4-year period. Anaconda would retain 49% ownership, and it said it planned to continue a mine expansion program.

Government assumption of control over some of Mexico's leading business enterprises during the previous 15 months was reported by the *N.Y. Times* Apr. 15, 1972. Among the companies were the country's largest hotel and newspaper chains and one of Mexico City's leading independent TV stations. No political or ecnomic plan was thought to be involved in the take-overs. All the companies concerned were caught in a credit squeeze and owed the government large sums.

(The government was planning to reorient mining production toward the needs of domestic industry rather than foreign consumers, it was reported. A government official had said that Mexico was almost completely self-sufficient in metals and minerals.)

The expropriation of several large private estates, totalling some 222,000 hectares, and their distribution among 941 peasant families, was reported in July 1972. The land was owned by some of the country's leading families. Among owners of the expropriated estates were Miguel Borunda, brother of a former governor of Chihuahua state; Sen. Manuel Guzman Willys, a former deputy minister of agriculture and descendants of Gen. Jesus Gajardo, assassin of revolutionary peasant leader Emiliano Zapata. Many of the estates, like Gajardo's, had been built up during the revolution of 1910-7.

The government nationalized the tobacco industry in Nov. 1972 and set up a new concern, Tabamex, to run it. The state held 52% of the new company's shares, peasant growers 24%, and private interests 24%. Tabamex received the wholesale monopoly of Mexican tobacco at home and abroad, although private companies were still able to manufacture cigars and cigarettes.

The government Aug. 16 had purchased 51% of the stock in Telefonos de Mexico, the national telephone company and the largest privately owned corporation in the country. Most of its stockholders were Mexican. Government control of the company reportedly caused concern among U.S. investors in Mexico, who feared nationalizations of foreign companies along Chilean lines. National Patrimony Min. Horacio Flores de la Pena asserted, however, that the government had not nationalized the phone company and would control but not administer the system. Flores added that stockholders would be permitted to keep their equity and that dividends would not be reduced.

With the takeover of the private Banco Internacional, the government announced in Sept. 1972 that it controlled 50% of all banking resources in the country.

Fresh tension developed between Mexico and the U.S. during 1972 over Mexico's treatment of foreign investors. U.S. Amb. Robert H. McBride expressed investors' complaints Oct. 12, charging that the Mexican government was trying to "change the rules of the game" with respect to the U.S.' $3 billion investment in the country. Industry & Commerce Undersecy. Jose Campillo Sainz confirmed that Mexico was changing the rules so that foreign investment would be accept-

able "when it accelerates and promotes our development
and conforms to the objectives we have outlined, without
ignoring the right of the investor to obtain a legitimate profit
on his investment." Echeverria charged Oct. 19 that there
was "great pressure for Mexican enterprises to keep selling
themselves to foreign interests" and that many companies
were being induced to import "useless technologies." His
Institutional Revolutionary Party Oct. 21 adopted declara-
tions condemning all forms of "imperialist manipulation"
and calling for nationalization of foreign enterprises.

Echeverria, however, encouraged foreigners to lease and
develop coastal and border land. (The previous government
had expropriated all foreign-owned coastal and border land.)
Echeverria May 1, 1972 had issued a presidential decree that
would permit legal, direct foreign participation in tourist and
industrial development of Mexico's borders. The decree allowed the creation of trusts with foreign capital for the leas-
ing of land within 33 miles of the coast and 66 miles of the
borders. It prohibited outright ownership of the land by foreigners but permitted them to utilize property in projects
approved by the Foreign Ministry.

The state oil concern Pemex contracted a U.S. engineering firm to design and build a petroleum refining plant cost-
ing about $50 million, it was reported Sept. 29, 1972. (Pemex
was reported June 8, 1973 to have found large oil deposits in
the Gulf of Mexico off the coast of Tabasco.)

The Mexican Congress in Feb. 1973 approved a moderate but controversial government bill regulating foreign investment. U.S. investors had opposed some of the bill's provisions, but the government claimed they entailed no substantial change in economic policy. The bill required that:
foreign investors complement Mexican capital rather than
displace it; open new fields of business and industrial activity;
mix their capital with Mexican capital; give Mexican citizens
first opportunity for available jobs and use foreign techniques
and employes on a limited basis; share advanced technology
and improved technical methods with Mexico; produce goods
for export; use domestic products and raw materials as much

as possible; and use foreign financing rather than make demands on limited Mexican credit. The non-retroactive bill was the first to control the extent and nature of foreign capital invested in Mexico. Foreign investment was currently estimated at $3.2 billion to $3.5 billion, about 80% of which was U.S. capital. According to government sources, foreign capital represented about 8% of its private investment and about 5% of its total investment.

Mexican authorities had charged that the planned withdrawal from Mexico of H. J. Heinz Co., the U.S. food processing firm, was a reaction against the foreign investment bill. Heinz, however, said it would withdraw because of "low returns." The Mexicans charged that Heinz had bought its way into the country at a "ridiculously low price" 9 years previously and had neglected the land on which it grew its crops.

A new company was formed with West German and Mexican capital in early 1973 to market public sector products internationally. The new firm, Exmex, planned to concentrate on basic commodities and railway rolling stock. It would operate on a worldwide basis, but would be concerned first with solving the imbalance of trade between Mexico and West Germany.

Japan's Mitsubishi Corp. announced in Tokyo in Apr. 1973 that it had purchased Exportadora de Sal, a salt manufacturing company in Mexico, from National Bulk Carriers Inc. of the U.S. for about $20 million. Mitsubishi said Exportadora had an annual production capacity of 4.5 million tons of salt, of which 2.8 million tons had been exported to Japan.

The National Bank warned in Feb. 1973 that Mexican industry would spend $670 million to import machine tools over the next decade unless a local machine tool industry began to develop.

Index

167